Think with the Heart
Love with the Mind

ACCELERATING YOUR INNER GROWTH

Paul Dugliss, M.D.

Cover Design: Paul Dugliss

Cover Image Credits:
>Abstract Heart: Bobbie Sandlin @ 123RF.com
>Beautiful Painting Goddess Woman with Ornamental Mandala: Jozef Klopacka @ 123RF.com
>Telepathy: Andrea Danti @ 123RF.com

For more information: www.pauldugliss.com

Table of Contents

Gratitude

The many blessings of my life, the ability to write this book, and the profound experiences I have had are the result of the grace of my amazing friends and teachers. Indeed, these teachings are universal truths that came from them and are now coming through me to you. It is with a heart full of gratitude that I acknowledge all my teachers and friends, especially Laszlo Sute, Janice Kinney, Charlie Lutes, Gil Eastin, Aureya Magdalen, Maharishi Mahesh Yogi, Alan Watts, Verlyn McGilvray and my dear brother Bill. I thank Charlie Lutes for the teaching and the title of the book. Deepest love and gratitude and all credit to David McClanahan, who has guided and fostered my growth and development ever since the day we met. Infinite appreciation and infinite gratitude to all those who have loved me and called me friend — your love has meant everything to me.

Part 1

The Foundations of Life and Love

My Promise

My life is proof that your biggest dreams are way too small. At every stage of my life, unimaginable experiences manifest. With each stage come profound realizations… With each a profound shift in my daily experience of life… With each, an increasing awe and love for all that is life... And finally, with each, untold inner and outer success — beyond anything you could imagine.

I could not imagine that I would be writing these words. I could not imagine that I would ever be experiencing a profound knowingness with each moment. I could not imagine being at peace with my brother's death, my mother's Alzheimer's, my father's aging or the atrocities of the world. I could not imagine finding love in each moment and seeing love in each person. But I am getting ahead of myself. For what I want for you is to go even beyond what I have experienced.

Open to this: You can expect more. You can be more. Actor and comedian Jim Carrey said this:

So many of us choose our path out of fear disguised as practicality. What you really want seems impossibly out of reach and ridiculous to expect, so you never dare to ask the universe for it. I'm saying that I'm the proof that you can ask the universe for it.

Jim Carrey had asked for 10 million dollars. He wrote himself a check for it and dated it at a time when he was an unsuccessful, starving comedian. He received 10 million for his role in *Dumb and Dumber* almost to the day of the date written on the check. He is proof of what you can ask the universe for. I am proof that your dreams and expectations of how you live and experience life are way too small.

While this may intrigue your mind, I call to your heart. I put forth to your heart the call to peace, the call to love, the call to effortlessness. I put forth the call to find a way of grace and ease. If you have been struggling so with life, my friend, let yourself rest now. The searching is over and the finding has begun. Rest in the knowledge that if it can unfold for me, with all the stress and winding twists and turns I have traveled, it certainly can unfold for you. All is to be unfolded here, and all grace is to be given to you. This is to be the way for you now. No more suffering. You will be led out of that. It will not happen suddenly, but can happen quickly. Suffering serves no one. It has been enough. Let the ease come. Let the healing begin.

Know that as you read these words, much is being conveyed to your subconscious mind. There is a part of you that will resonate with what I am saying, just as a guitar string will resonate with a pure voice and vibrate without being strummed. Grace is here. Grace is present and brings forth a transformation within you that will allow you to become aware of the truth in these words. It will allow you to become aware of the possibility that your life can now make a dramatic turn — one that is so much better than before. Your well-being, your innermost being, resonates with this idea. It wakes up to this idea. Increased awareness brings increased light. It brings an enlightenment, as enlightenment usually happens gradually with each slight increase in light. This is worth celebrating.

I want you to see and know that a shift is taking place within you. Your mind will need to let go of much, but your heart will be filled much at the same time. At times, your mind will make it out to be the hardest thing in the world — but then it will become clear and real, and as natural and easy as breathing.

The time has come.

It is not the grace of a master, nor the grace of a teacher, nor the grace of some external God that frees you. It is the grace of the purity that exists deep within your heart. It is the innocent depth of your own heart and its inherent connection to something greater that will provide the grace that holds the key. It is love that frees you. It is love that creates the ease. And this love is larger and more powerful than anything you have experienced. But once again, I am getting ahead of myself. For now, dear friend, just be open.

I am asking you to open to a greater understanding, to one fundamental truth: What works at one level of development doesn't work at another. When a billionaire talks about how to gain money and refers to investments and hedge funds, that wisdom doesn't apply to those of us who live paycheck to paycheck.

If you long for inner freedom, if you long for higher consciousness, if you long for love and bliss, if you long for ease and success in life, then understand that the keys to your growth and your fastest inner development are described here. No longer does it suffice to adopt the ways of the East. No longer does it suffice for us to meditate for 20 or 30 years to achieve freedom. A faster way is available now. And it can be full of ease.

I pray this: May my words inspire you. May my words bring healing energy to you. May my words comfort you. May my words open your heart. May my words touch your heart. May the opening of your heart and your mind bring fulfillment to you. May my words bring love to your life. May my words bring awe and amazement. May my words create the cherishing of each moment of your life. And most of all, may my words heal your heart.

I pray that you be in the experience of love — that you sit in the fullness of your wonderful and tender heart. I pray that you come to know the power of love — the incredible strength it holds. I long for this for you and for all of humanity. How to get there? It is not a matter of will. It is not a matter of belief. It is not a matter of understanding or insight. It is the result of growth: inner growth, human growth, the growth you were designed for as an adult — full and complete human development.

I have outlined the keys to accelerating this growth and development in this book. My promise to you: If you use these techniques, if you practice them regularly, if you follow the advice here, you will dramatically improve your life. You will be happier, healthier and, above all, you will find more love and fulfillment in your life. And you will eventually awaken to attain a more enlightened life. I can guarantee you that. What I can't guarantee is the timing. You have your own rate of growth as you did in puberty. I can know what will be, but I am always aware it is on God's timing.

One of my favorite jokes is about the man who seeks a conversation with God. He goes to the Himalayas and finds a sage and asks him, "How can I have a conversation with God?"

The sage replies, "Near the top of this mountain is a cave. Meditate in it for 10 years. After 10 years go to the top of the mountain, and God will appear and grant you a question."

The man goes into the cave and meditates for 10 years, and 10 years to the day he goes to the top of the mountain. The heavens part, and God appears and says, "My son, you have meditated well. What is your question?"

"God, is it true that an entire human lifetime is but a second to you?"

"Yes, my son, it is true: An entire human lifetime is but a second to me."

The man goes back down the mountain and back to his cave and meditates another 10 years. Ten years to the day he goes back to the top of the mountain. The heavens part.

"My son, you have meditated well. What is your question?"

"God, is it true that all the wealth in the world is but a dime to you?"

"Yes, my son, it is true: All the wealth in the world is but a dime to me."

The man goes back down the mountain and back to his cave and meditates another 10 years. Now he is getting pretty old, but 10 years to the day he goes back to the top of the mountain. The heavens part.

"My son, you have meditated well. What is your question?"

"God, can you spare a dime?"

There is a pause.

"Why certainly," comes the reply. "Just a second."

Things happen on the Divine's timing, not ours. And God is so very patient and waits for us to wake up to the truth of life. You do wake up eventually. With this book and these methods, it will happen in less than a second.

My promise to you, my friend, is that if you follow this path based in love, your life will transform in ways you never could have imagined and you will live beyond your wildest dreams. May my words inspire you, and may you be so blessed.

"

If you follow this path based in love, your life will

transform in ways you never could have imagined.

"

Out of Darkness

When I was young boy, I was aware that two-thirds of the world went to bed hungry at night. Although very middleclass, I was well aware of the privileged life I had. In many ways, I experienced a deep sadness about the world. Perhaps it was like a survivor's grief — feeling that any money that my parents spent on my education could have been spent feeding the starving in other countries. Many lives could have been saved, if I were not there.

Later, in high school, I left home to go to a private school. Overworking, no longer being one of the smartest in the class (a major difference between the public and private school), beginning to question the purpose of life and getting depressed with the craziness of the world, I fell into depression. I felt the world would be better off without me. My teachers became aware of my depression and morbid thoughts and set me up with a counselor.

After a couple of months, I still was confused about the purpose of life. Why was there so much suffering, and how I could continue to tap out my parent's budget going to an expensive school, even though I received a scholarship? The school counselor recommended I see a psychiatrist, who frankly was a waste of time. The more I asked about the purpose of life, the more he changed the subject. If I started to get emotional, he decided to play checkers with me. I was seeking answers to what life was about, and he thought playing checkers would help me.

The psychiatrist's office was about three miles from the school. My counselor or one of the teachers would drive me there and pick me up. I was still trying to understand life and how people worked. This one session — I believe it was the next to last session — my ride did not show to pick me up after my appointment. After waiting for almost 25 minutes, I decided I would have to walk back to the school. I had not planned on walking, so I had worn my dress shoes. I had not gotten a half a mile when the sidewalk ended, and I began to walk in the grass median between the three lanes of traffic on either side of the road. The sky clouded over and I decided I needed to run if I was going to have any chance of beating the rain. Within two minutes of starting to run, torrential rain poured down on me.

Here I was running in the warm rain, the sound of the cars plowing through the water loudly on both sides of me, my clothes getting soaked. The running, the rain, and the noise all brought me out of the mind and into a state of exhilaration that simultaneously thrilled and baffled me. This should have been a terrible day, a terrible thing — look at all that had gone wrong. My ride never showed, the psychiatrist wasted my time and my parents' money, the rain was soaking my clothes, and I was running in my dress shoes. And yet I was exhilarated. The exertion and the sound and the warm rain thrilled me. I felt awe and wonder in that moment.

In the transcendence of the mind came the realization, the intuition, the knowing: Happiness is the purpose of life. The banker is happy making money, the doctor is happy saving lives, and the priest saves souls because that is what makes him happy. Each person undertakes his or her path because they are drawn to the happiness it brings. Much later I realized that "happiness" is not a fleeting emotion but rather what comes when you do what you love doing. It is a form of love that is created when you fulfill your purpose — a special love that brings joy and fulfillment. This is why you are here — to find what you love and bring that into the world.

While my understanding of this love continued to evolve and grow, what I recognized only later was the special nature of the moment of realization. At the time of the realization, I was so relieved and still so identified with my thoughts that I did not ponder how they came to be — what caused me to have this realization. Something special had happened. My life had been transformed. My depression lifted, even if my cynicism about the world would persist for a few years more. And, unbeknownst to me, the deep impression of that moment of transcendence stayed with me and became something I would seek consciously in a couple of years.

This moment in my life has been a rich source of understanding. It demonstrated to me a key principle and much of the point of this book: We don't solve problems — we outgrow them. In that moment of greater awareness, I was able to step out of the mind. I now understand that this is how we grow. In a moment of greater awareness, we transform and integrate that higher awareness into our perspective and functioning.

"

We don't solve problems — we outgrow them.

"

Years later, through studying neuroanatomy, I came to understand that the left brain is where logic and analysis reside. The right brain is where intuition and the ability to perceive holistic patterns reside. In the moment when I let go and experienced the sensations of the rain on my skin, the sound of the tires of the cars in the rain, the feeling of my breath and the exhilaration of my body, my left brain quieted. My right brain was primed for the intuition that I would have. The greater awareness of life and what was real was integrated with my quest for understanding, and I saw so deeply into life that it transformed my depression and my life.

One other related key to growth came decades later: The functioning of the brain must be integrated. The running set up the alternating use of one side of the brain and then the other, allowing for better communication and integration of the two sides of the brain. It brought a quicker integration of the insight. Bottom line: Optimizing the functioning of the human nervous system is key to growth.

This for me, like for many, was the beginning of what is called the spiritual path. Seeking to understand suffering in order to find a way out is a common way that people are brought to spirituality — to seeking something more in life.

Whether it is out of pain, out of someone's love for you or out of your own inner curiosity and wisdom, you open to the possibility that there is something more to life than work, family, making money and eating good food.

"

Whether it is out of pain or out of someone's love for you, you open to the possibility that there is something more to life.

"

While this is said to be the beginning of the "spiritual path," it is really just the normal function of adult growth. This is the beginning of inner growth. This is what is necessary for growth. This is why it takes no effort. Your normal state as a child was to be open to learning and growing. It actually takes effort to close yourself to that. If it has become your habit to close yourself to growth and change, to no longer wonder or expect more in life, then it will take effort to break through that. But it will be well worth it. Otherwise, understand that the seeking is coming to an end, and the finding is beginning. That is normal. It is human. It is human growth and development. And it is yours to have.

"

Understand that the seeking is coming to an end, and the finding is beginning.

"

Watering the Root

How do you grow? How do you understand what awaits you when you open to that "something more"? For me, the next step was major. My wonderful brother Bill was also seeking something greater in life, and he jumped into philosophy and started feeding me books to read. One that stood out was *The Master Game* by William De Ropp. Like my own realization, De Ropp talked about the various purposes or "games" humans play in order to find happiness. He sectioned these into lower games like "Cock on a Dunghill," played for fame and one-upmanship. The middle game was described as the Householder Game, played to raise a family and continue the species. The higher games are played for things like salvation (the Religion Game) or beauty (the Art Game). But then he described a game of games, which is above even the higher, nobler games. He called this the Master Game, explaining that it is about awakening out of the illusion of all the games. He described how experts at the Master Game saw normal waking life as a dream that anyone can awaken from, just like you awake from dreams at night.

I was sold. I wanted to awaken. The book revealed the key to this awakening: meditation or the states that martial arts masters attain through their practices. I decided I would learn to meditate, and I would learn a martial art. Little did I think of my earlier realization and the fact that it had come from an almost-meditative state.

At first, I tried to meditate on my own. De Ropp had mentioned silencing the mind. I lived by the mind. This was the hardest thing for me to do. I tried staring at the wall. My mind would wander from one location of the wall to another. I tried staring at a point in the grain in the door. Try as I might, I could not stop my mind. I tried timing it. Maybe 10 seconds at the most. If this was meditation, I was a colossal failure at it. How does anyone stop the mind? I felt lost.

Shortly thereafter, a dear friend from across the street and I started talking. I told him about the book and about my decision to learn to meditate and learn a martial art. He laughed: "Funny, you should say that. I just learned to meditate. You should learn. I think they have a lecture next week at the public library." I asked him if he could meditate. "Sure, it's easy." I was envious. I had tried and failed. I didn't think that it could be easy for me.

Growth of awareness, developing a greater style of functioning of the brain, requires some input from the environment. This is the same for children when they grow, even for kittens. For example, if a kitten is put into an environment with all vertical lines while its nervous system is developing, then it will not be able to see horizontal lines when it becomes a cat. It will trip over cracks in the sidewalk. Fortunately for us, our brains are a bit more flexible, and you can accelerate your growth with this input at almost any age after age 10 — the point at which you have the capability to examine your thoughts.

Growth is not a mystery. You need to change your brain, and you do this by watering it at the root, as you would a plant. The root, the basis, is rest. Resting the brain, both right and left hemispheres, is the key to accelerating growth. It is the key to growing awareness. It is the key to developing consciousness. Awareness is the water — pure awareness. The deep rest of the mind in meditation is watering the root functioning of the nervous system.

My first meditation experience was telling. I was interested in meditation to understand reality and higher consciousness. When I heard the instructor talk of all the practical aspects of meditation and the research substantiating it, I was impressed. By the time he started talking about cosmic consciousness and world peace, I felt he was off track, too far out there. I had forgotten the very purpose that brought me to formal meditation instruction! That is how unclear I was.

I had already tried concentration techniques, so the first formal meditation instruction that I had was in Transcendental Meditation, even though today I teach Heart-based Meditation. Those first meditation experiences were such a contrast for me that I will never forget them. My mind was all over the place prior to learning. When the instructor started chanting a preparation chant, I felt a wave of fear come over me. What was this, some kind of cult? I decided to look for the shortest path to the door. But then I thought, "I can always leave," and decided to just put up with the ceremony.

All of that worry disappeared after my first meditation. After the initial instruction, I was led into a small room with a window to the outside. It was July, so it was quite warm, and the window was open. I followed the instructions and began to meditate on my own for the first time. During the meditation my mind began to settle, and I felt an incredible peace come over me. It seemed as if time stood still for a moment, and a deep relaxation and letting go took place, leaving my mind like a placid lake. When the instructor told me to take some time to come out of the meditation, I was amazed. I could hear sounds out the window, but it was like the first time I had ever heard sound. Everything was so clear, so settled, so clean and crisp. Colors were so bright. It was as if I had never seen before.

The next months became a fascinating story of growth for me. With no reference point, I had no idea how overactive my mind was. From the silence of meditation, I became aware of many things that I just took for granted. My dreams went from chaotic, fragmented snippets to reflections of the day I had just had or intuitions about the coming day. My memory became clearer. I could clearly remember why I had started meditating.

It is hard to describe the changes that took place in even the first few months. I went from an agnostic view of the world to a profound reverence for life and an awareness of the divinity within all of nature and all the world. I could not become depressed for any significant amount of time. Each meditation seemed to wipe the slate clean, and I was ready to start anew. I felt an aliveness I had never felt before. I had incredible interest in everything and overloaded my schedule during my first year of college.

While the meditations varied from session to session, that same crispness and awe and clarity would come to me time and time again. I truly looked forward to each meditation. It was my twice-daily vacation that allowed me to come back to my life refreshed, excited, focused and openhearted. Words cannot describe the experience. It is as if I had been set totally free from every worry, every concern, every pain, every problem and given a chance to reside in pure bliss.

Through great blessings and grace I had been given the most important tool in unfolding and accelerating inner growth — the gift of an effortless meditation technique. At each phase of growth you need certain inputs to the brain in order to reach the next stage of development. I had stumbled into the exact input needed at that point in my life.

Growth is not a mystery. It is concrete with specific requirements. And this type of growth can result in an awesome and mystical wonderment that makes life a breathtaking adventure.

❝

Growth is not a mystery, but it can result in a profoundly mystical, awe-inspired life.

❞

I was so blessed and so lucky that I had stumbled into one of the most advanced and rapid methods of meditation. The problem with the word "meditation" is that people have the concept that everything labeled meditation is the same. Not so. There are probably three fundamental classes of meditation that have profoundly different effects on the brain.

Class 1: Controlled Focus or Concentration

Classic examples of concentration or controlled focus are found in the revered traditions of Zen, Tibetan Buddhism, Qigong, yoga and Vedanta, which involve attempts to control or direct the mind. Attention is focused on an object of meditation — such as one's breath, an idea or image, or an emotion (loving compassion would be an example). Brainwaves recorded during these practices are typically in the gamma frequency (20-50 Hz), seen whenever you concentrate or during "active" cognitive processing. Gamma waves are associated with high levels of focus and concentration, which can lead to more heightened "presence."

Class 2: Open Monitoring

These styles are where the content of the mind is allowed to come and go without judgment or evaluation or involvement. This includes Mindfulness Meditation, Vipassana Meditation, some Qigong and some yoga meditations. This style of meditation produces frontal theta brainwaves that are associated with creativity, dreaming, intuition, memory tasks or reflection on mental concepts.

Class 3: Automatic Self-transcending

These styles involve practices that are designed for the process to go beyond itself — beyond its own mental activity. This allows the mind to spontaneously go beyond the process of meditation itself. These approaches are effortless. Examples of this include Transcendental Meditation, Primordial Sound Meditation, Sahaj Samadhi Meditation, certain Christian mystic meditations and Heart-based Meditation. The brainwave pattern associated with this is frontal alpha-wave coherence, which is associated with deep states of relaxation with inner wakefulness.

All of that is very technical stuff. The bottom line is this: With the automatic self-transcending style of meditation, you actually rest the nervous system deeply and *grow* consciousness, grow awareness and increase the power of thought. At the point of deepest rest, maximum coherence between the hemispheres of the brain exists. With the other methods you *refine* how you are using the consciousness you have. One style grows awareness; the others mainly integrate the awareness that you already have. Both can lead to the same place with enough time, but the automatic self-transcending methods are faster. I have tried all three styles of meditation, and the advantage of the last is not just that it rapidly grows awareness, but that it is easy to do. Many people try concentration and open monitoring techniques and find them hard to do. I had lucked out and fallen into something that would transform my life that didn't require much effort on my part.

I can't emphasize enough the depth of misunderstanding and confusion around meditation, inner growth and development. Please note the distinction here. One style of meditation is for rapidly expanding awareness and other styles are for integrating that awareness into our mental, emotional and energetic functioning — for transforming our perception of reality. Many of the problems in understanding complete human development come from this misconception. Understand the history. Many of the open monitoring and concentration techniques originated in monk traditions. Monks meditated long hours a day and needed focus. They needed to integrate. They needed to be present. This got mistaken for the whole thing. It is not. You need both a method of developing greater awareness and a method of integrating it into your life, your personality patterns, your style of thinking, etc. These need to be based on Western methods for the householder, not Eastern methods for the monk.

I want to convey to you the importance of sorting out the confusion around inner growth and development. Nothing is more important at this juncture in history. We are literally dying because we, as a society, do not know how to grow and use our full potential. We don't know how to solve our problems. But you deserve to know. You deserve a chance to be all that you can be.

The problem with the self-transcending style of meditation is that it is often touted as "The Answer." It is the most important part of the foundation of growth. It is the water to the root. You need to expand awareness. But the plant still needs sunshine. You need to integrate and upgrade your patterns based on this expanded awareness. You need both water and sunshine.

"

Meditation is the foundation of inner growth.

"

One of the things that slowed my inner growth and development was this notion that all that was necessary to grow and know reality, to experience the highest human development, was to meditate regularly. I did this almost religiously, not because I was particularly disciplined, rather because it made me feel and function better. I did not miss a single day's meditation in all of medical school, for example. But here was my mistake. I meditated and then undid most of the progress during my day. Meditation is like taking a bath. You won't be very clean if you jump out the bath and roll in the mud. I overworked my nervous system with the stress of medical school and residency, difficult relationships and self-doubts, and self-destructive emotional patterns. I took on way too much and tried to keep pace with students 15 years my junior. Even before medical school, this was my habit — to overdo and engage in emotional patterns that were self-defeating.

The blessings of my life were that along the way I met the most evolved and enlightened friends who steered me toward greater growth. They offered me the keys to integration. I only took a few decades to realize it. The blessings of these friends and the great blessing of a patient Creator allowed me to struggle and discover the principles of accelerated inner growth.

To summarize, there are two parts to growth — expansion and integration.

The integration facet I began to explore through these blessed friends. They taught me well with such compassion and patience. Decades later the things they taught me led me to understand how to *integrate* the greater awareness resulting from meditation. My development, like yours, has these two parts. As the process goes back and forth from expansion to integration, I will also go back and forth in explaining them.

Let me also explain that having an effortless, easy meditation technique is key. Those in the world need a meditation style that gives them a break from their day — not another difficult task.

Heart-based Meditation is not only easy, but it also cultivates the heart and the joy in life. Many of the integration techniques (like mindfulness) are focused more on the mind than the heart. These types of meditation technique that come from monk traditions are often hard to stay with. Heart-based Meditation becomes an enjoyable practice that makes one feel better. It becomes easy to do day after day. It also provides the fuel for the process of integration and the many techniques and realizations that I owe to the gifts of my amazing friends.

Laszlo

One of my first teachers was named Laszlo. He was a very short, round Hungarian immigrant who had a floral and gift shop. His shop was filled with gnomes and fairy trinkets, and he had an almost gnome-like appearance. When I was introduced to him, my friend said, "Laszlo is very close to nature. The squirrels and birds will come and eat out his hand." It was true. Laszlo had a marvelously joyous radiance. It was the first time I could feel a deep peacefulness emanating from a human being — a feeling I would later recognize around other very developed individuals.

Laszlo would always give me a flower to take home, every time I visited his store. And he would always give me a smile. Laszlo was the first person I ever met who could read auras and intuitively know things about me that I had never told anyone.

Laszlo was a great teacher in *who he was*. He emanated love, something everyone including the animals picked up on. He liked to laugh. He used to joke that he was an angel who got booted out of heaven for being so mischievous, and that he was.

Laszlo challenged my limited view of the world. Whether it was politics or sex, he had a unique and often humorous take on things that challenged me to think bigger and definitely outside the box. I used to take him out for lunch. The only place we could find anything vegetarian was at a Taco Bell. We sat in that Taco Bell talking for hours at a time.

One day Laszlo took me to a picnic table behind his store and said, "You have been meditating long enough. You should be able to see auras by now. Let me show you how." We meditated together, and then he started trying to teach me how to look past things and not focus on them. He was trying to show me how to use the awareness I had been developing. I had great expectations and excitement when he made his announcement. But unfortunately, I could only see an occasional glimpse of some white light and I thought it was just an afterimage. Later in my life, I recognized that I actually had seen more than I realized — that my expectations were in the way. It was the beginning of using my expanded awareness.

Laszlo was also pivotal in one of the key realizations of my life — a realization that everyone comes to as they develop themselves. We are not the body, and we do go on after the body ceases.

While before my experience of running in the rain I had wished for death, after it, that was all changed. I suddenly became concerned that I would die and way too early. Shortly thereafter, I was riding in a plane, and some turbulence came along. I began to wonder what would happen if the plane went down. It was the first and only time I was ever afraid in an airplane. I did not want my life to end. I was afraid it might end all too quickly. This fear of death was something that disappeared completely and forever the more I talked with Laszlo.

Laszlo always rearranged my view of the world. The problem was that he was so mischievous that I had a hard time sorting out what was real and what was a joke. It was easy for my mind to discount what seemed outlandish as him trying to stir the pot and not as something deep and meaningful. So when Laszlo first explained reincarnation to me, I took it with a grain of salt.

One of the first things Laszlo told me about my past lives was that I had spent many, many lifetimes as a monk. And that in this lifetime I was not to be a monk because it was important for me to be in the world, helping people and enjoying life, including sex. I wondered if it were true. Why lifetimes as a monk? Why not as a teacher or a doctor or a housewife or a thief? A year later I met an amazing intuitive named Jan, and the first thing she said to me was, "You've spent lifetimes as a monk." I was taken aback. The first two people I knew who said they could see past lives had told me the exact same thing. They did not know each other. They had not asked me any questions about myself, and they both said the exact same thing. I had to pause. I started to think about this. All of science is based on the ability to reproduce observations. If you do an experiment correctly you should be able to observe the same results. Laszlo and Jan had observed the same thing with their higher awareness. My mind could find no explanation for this. This was not a coincidence. It was not a matter of believing. I could not refute what had happened. I had to consider the possibility that reincarnation was real and that as we grow and develop we can know these details firsthand.

One other comment stands out. At the time I met Laszlo, I was working as a master's level psychologist on a psych ward. I remember him talking about reincarnation and my future. Except for a fleeting month or two in the first year of college, I had never considered becoming a doctor, and, with my work in psychology, it was the furthest thing from my mind. At one point, he looked up at me with his sweet, mischievous smile and said, "In your next lifetime you will be an Ayurvedic doctor. Maybe even in this lifetime." I laughed. It sounded way too far-fetched, but that is what happened.

It is one thing to have a belief or visit a psychic for entertainment. It is quite another thing to have a direct experience of being separate from the body in meditation and having two distinct people observe the exact same thing about your past lives. Again, I had missed the full opportunity to integrate these realizations. The techniques for doing so would come later, as I began working with Jan and other intuitives on my growth and development.

The point is that belief is one thing. The last thing we need is a New Age religion based on belief. Experience is what is needed — not new concepts and beliefs, not faith and mental concepts. These experiences were both exciting and shocking for me. They woke me up to a greater reality. I write about them not so that you believe in such things, rather that you get inspired to grow and discover them for yourself through your own experience. When you do, your perspectives on life will change dramatically — not because you believe, rather because you *know based on your experience*. Growth allows us to *know* reality more accurately, not *believe* it is a certain way. With this growth and development, religious wars would become a thing of the past.

As I grew and integrated these experiences, any fear of death disappeared completely. Obviously, I would be sad if I didn't have the opportunity to finish my life, but I realized quite clearly that the body dies, not me. I go on. As I integrated this knowledge, it helped me to understand some of the weird patterns I seem to have been born with. It helped me understand why I felt and experienced life the way I did as a child. I had often experienced myself being awake with no awareness of the body in meditation. Integrating that awareness into my thinking and outlook on the world resulted in my fear of death being gone completely. Strangely enough, while before my experience of running in the rain, I felt the world would be better off without me… after the experience, I became afraid of dying. Through Laszlo's love and laughter and his bold description of reality, fearlessness became my reality. The awareness I had in meditation of myself separate from the body integrated with a higher understanding of the trajectory of my soul and both reincarnation and freedom from fear of death became my reality.

Expanding awareness and integrating that awareness into one's thinking and perspective and emotional patterns — these are the two facets of growth. For one you need self-transcending meditation. For the other you need integration techniques. These were to start with the knowledge, wisdom and techniques I learned from Jan.

Jan

The process of inner growth involves the cultivation of greater awareness. The infusion of greater consciousness and higher vibration into the human nervous system, like pouring electricity into a wire, allows this greater awareness to be experienced and held. This then needs to be integrated with all of the patterns of the mind, the emotions, and the energy field of the body. When this integration takes place, there is a marked shift in experience, and this often accompanied by a realization.

❝

The process of inner growth involves cultivation of greater awareness.

❞

You will go through certain realizations as you grow. These realizations result from you being more in touch with what is ultimately real in life. It is one thing to read about realizations. It is another to experience them. The experience is the result of the integration of greater awareness into your ego structures, your energetic structure and your mental perceptions. And you can accelerate this process. Meditation forms the foundation — the expansion of awareness. Energy work enhances the integration process. Affirmations and visualizations enhance the shifts in the mind and in the emotional body. Many other techniques are involved, but they all fall into integrating awareness on one level or another of our being.

I had become an avid fan of meditation through my experience with Transcendental Meditation. The TM teachers shunned psychological and psychic exploration. The attitude was that these things are not necessary, that all you need is regular meditation. I sensed that this was not true. I know now that what is needed is a means for integrating the greater awareness and for further accelerating the growth. At the time, I simply had a desire to learn and grow, and so, against the advice of many teachers, I went to visit a very wise intuitive named Jan.

By the time I had met her I had had many "mystical" experiences. In meditation I would often feel myself enter into a state of timelessness and lose track of my body as I went deep within. I often felt as large as the universe. I experienced myself as something other than the body and had a feeling of universality. I had had some experiences of being "out of the body" and had experience the feeling of being united with everything — that I was everything. I took these as experiences that were wonderful, but my mind separated them from my daily experience. I had had several clairvoyant dreams, so when I heard that Jan could know things about you intuitively, I was very open and interested. Jan had offered a Dharmic reading. I understood Dharma to be the purpose of one's life, particularly one's career. At that time I was working as a software engineer and wondering what my true calling was. So I was intrigued when I heard about the offer of a Dharmic reading, even if it was frowned upon by the Transcendental Meditation teachers.

My first meeting shook up so much of what I had assumed. It could not help but shake things up. My concept of Dharma and life purpose was far too naive. Jan explained that the soul is here to learn certain lessons that had been mapped out prior to the start of the life. These major lessons could be in almost any career, so my concern with choosing one particular one was misguided. She jumped into the major lessons I was here to learn. She spoke with enthusiasm and certainty, and she had a piercing gaze with her intense blue eyes. She talked as if she had known me all my life. She talked about my childhood. She talked about my shyness and how I was to be open and sharing with everyone in an expansive, expressive manner. She spoke about how it was my turn to be the authority and make decisions that affected others' lives — that it was like having to give a speech at school after everyone else had gone, and it was my turn. Minute after minute she pegged my greatest dilemmas and told me about my inner psychology; something that took me aback with its accuracy. And then she started talking about my sex life and what was happening internally for me. She explained how it was working against what I came here to learn and how to shift it so that the sex life became more an expression of the love that I am. At that point the alarm bells went off. "Is nothing private?" I wondered. Obviously not. Very obviously not.

It was then that I realized the experiences of expanding outside of the body meant both that I could sense and feel and communicate with others on the inner planes and they with me. Nothing was really private. While many psychics have indicated to me that there needs to be permission on the soul level for things to be shared, my experience drove home the point that all is available to everyone. While I had a sense that our thoughts and feelings and energies affect others and might be read or sensed by others, I now knew that everyone is connected — even more connected than most realize. Nothing is private. You can't hide things. Not that I had that much to hide, but like everyone, I was very sensitive about my insecurities and mistakes.

I thought deeply on this point. What a different world it would be if people only knew that whatever they thought or did or felt was forever written in the ethers for anyone to see. Who would think negatively about another soul? Who would ever cheat or do something illegal? If everyone were to grow to the point where they *realized* this truth, not just believed it to be true, how would the world change?

The concept of nothing being private might scare you. "How is that growth?" you might ask. Because you realize that we all carry shame and self-doubt, and we don't have to think of ourselves as different and needing to hide that. Because you realize that truth is real. "The truth will out." It always gets known in the end, either during in this life or at its end. And because it inspires you to be real — always.

"

What a different world it would be if people only knew that whatever they thought or did or felt was forever written in the ethers for anyone to see.

"

While the experience with Jan offered me a huge realization, she also taught me several very important techniques for integration. When I practiced them after meeting her, I saw dramatic changes. It was my own lack of clarity about growth and the doubts I had from some of the meditation teachers that allowed me to overlook the great gifts she had given. I had to reclaim them much later in life when I was no longer doing Transcendental Meditation and had forged ahead with Heart-based Meditation.

The Key to Everything

My heart says, "I am sorry for your pain and suffering."
My mind says, "This is not necessary."
My inspiration says, "Humanity is ready to outgrow this."
My wisdom says, "Please let me show you the way — it is easier
than you think."

It *is* easier than you think because it is what is natural. You understand that houseplants need sunlight, water, air and moderate temperature to grow. What do you need to grow, especially after age 20?

You need two things: A way of increasing awareness and a way to integrate that awareness into your mental and emotional patterns.

The toughest challenges in life — making sense of how to navigate relationships, developing wealth and abundance — all of these are not a matter of greater knowledge. It is seldom that you don't have access to knowledge. What you need is growth. Most of your greatest challenges can't be solved through the power of intellect; most problems can be solved by outgrowing them.

As a teenager there is great worry about who is in the "in" crowd, how we will fit it, and whether we want to fit. As adults, we usually outgrow this. We don't sit down and worry about the "in" crowd and fitting in. You may say there are plenty of adults who still worry about fitting in. Understand many of us have our growth stunted. Many stop growing. Most people don't know how human adults grow and develop. Thus, the opportunity is lost, growth is stunted, and potential remains unrealized.

We all want more. We all seek greater happiness, greater fulfillment, greater success, greater health, greater love and greater spiritual connection. If we want these for ourselves, we must recognize a fundamental truth — that if you want to fulfill your full potential, you must keep growing.

There are many aspects of this growth. Growth is holistic. As you grow, you come to know and experience reality more accurately. The clarity of the mind grows. Equally as important is the growth of the heart. Until you are fully grown and have fully developed the heart's potential for love and joy, fulfillment is extremely limited.

Growth involves increasing awareness and integrating that awareness. This is not separate from changes in the nervous system. Too often inner development has gotten relegated to the category of New Age spirituality or mysticism. This is not so. This is an error of the mind. The mind can analyze, compartmentalize and separate everything. It is akin to watching the world through a slot in a picket fence as you walk by it. Behind it is an animal, a dog for example. First glance, you see a head. Second, you see nothing but picket fence. Third glance you see a tail. At a certain level of development (as a young child), you don't make any connection between the two. They are separate and distinct. You may even imagine that one causes the other to appear. "Head causes this thing, a tail, to appear." You see them as separate things, which perhaps have some connection. This is exactly the way many see and understand human growth. Most people see spiritual development, personal development, brain development, health, love and fulfillment as separate, distinct and disconnected things. But like the head and tail of the dog, they are all elements of the *same* thing. They occur when you grow past age 20.

At this time, a dramatic shift is needed for humanity. This shift does not come from technology. It does not come from economics. It does not come through religion or through trying to be a better person. Solving the problems of life — solving your problems — does not come with taking another course, changing your attitude or perspective, or sitting at the feet of a guru. Humanity's problems, like your problems, are solved in two ways: You focus on them and develop and implement strategies to solve them, or you outgrow them. Most of the problems of childhood that you have conquered you did so through growth, not through brute-force problem solving. The same is true for humanity. In order to go to the moon, we grew the computer industry. In order to feed the world, we grew new strains of wheat and other crops. The overthrow of many tyrannical governments in the Middle East has come through social media — through the growth of the Internet.

The greatest problem facing humanity is wasted potential. We have long known that humans use only a small amount of the brain's capacity. We have not long known how to use that capacity. *Now we know.*

"

The greatest problem facing humanity is wasted potential.

"

How do you use your full potential, and how do you outgrow your problems? Read on. Through this process you will discover the greatest love that you ever will experience. This is about what will transform all humanity. The useless conflicts, wars, terrorism and abuse of the environment are present as a result of humanity not utilizing its full potential and outgrowing its problems. The problems persist, not because we want them, rather simply because we do not use our brain's capacity to see a broader vision, to comprehend the long term consequences of our current actions, to understand what will bring success to all of us. Nothing is more important at this juncture than this knowledge of growth and development. A peaceful world starts with a peaceful individual. A fulfilled world starts with a fulfilled individual. A fully actualized world, starts with an individual whose potential is fully actualized.

Growth is powerful. One of my mentors in Ayurvedic Medicine used to tell a story of his patients in rural Virginia. My mentor had a combined rheumatology and internal medicine practice, so often the tobacco farmers would come see him for their annual checkups. One day a patient came in after having blood work done and said, "Well, doc, how am I doing?"

My mentor explained, "Everything looks great! All your labs are normal; your blood pressure is great — much better than before. I don't find anything on your physical exam. Whatever you are doing, keep doing it." My mentor had gotten this man to meditate the year before to keep his blood pressure normal, so he asked how it was going.

"Great, doc. I get it in every day, just like you told me."

"That's wonderful. Helps your blood pressure to stay normal. So, do you have any questions for me?"

This tobacco farmer looked uncomfortable for a moment and finally said, "Well doc, I do have one question that has been bothering me."

"What's that?"

"Doc, I keep forgetting to smoke. Is that all right?"

This tobacco farmer expected to want to smoke tobacco. As his awareness grew, he lost the taste for it. He became aware of its impact on his body and lost the desire to smoke. He kept forgetting to smoke, which made him wonder if something was wrong. My mentor reassured him that this was normal. This is what happens when we grow. We often outgrow old habits and patterns. In the transition it can be confusing, if we identified the habit as part of "us."

It all comes down to this fundamental truth: Growth does not stop at age 20. The lack of any cultural structure or framework or method of growth means the knowledge of how to grow has been lost. The result of not knowing how to grow to your full potential is what you see today: incredible fragmentation in society, inability to address huge problems, drug abuse, alcohol abuse, violence and killing with unbelievable frequency. I could go on and on.

Spiritual development is not separate from maturity. It is not separate from brain integration. It is not different from moral development. It is not separate from health and healthy relationships. It is not separate from love. The mind tends to make things separate. They all come as the result of growth, and this growth is reflected in the functioning of the brain. It is the growth that reflects in each of these facets. Yet, it is one diamond with many facets — human growth.

I was incredibly shy, as a young boy. I did not like to be in front of people. I hated performing, even though I liked music and sports. Even into my 20s, I carried this shyness. I felt challenged even later in medical school making rounds when the attending physician put me on the spot, asking me questions in front of the other residents and medical students. It was nerve-wracking and horrible for me to have to confront this on a daily basis. Then something happened in my second year of residency when I noticed it was simply gone. I was able to talk on any case or any subject and did not have any self-consciousness. I had simply outgrown my shyness. Today I love to speak in front of groups and spend a lot of my time teaching. You outgrow things if you open to growth and undertake to develop yourself.

"

A peaceful world starts with a peaceful individual.

"

This is the inside scoop that your parents and your society never told you: You are essentially designed for inner growth. Call that growth spiritual if you want. It is actually holistic. If you foster growth, you will grow in all areas, even in terms of spirituality. Spirituality has nothing to do with church or religion. It has to do with finding meaning in life. As you grow, you fulfill the human design. You are designed to assign meaning to things — to others' words and perceptions, to others' actions, to your actions and all the events and experiences in your life. It has to do with seeing the world completely — not as a head causing a tail. It has to do with *knowing reality completely*, not just believing what you have heard from religious or spiritual sources or even New Age teachers. It is not just a conceptual meaning; it is a direct knowing that comes as we grow further.

The quality of your life is dependent on your ability to fully know reality. If you assign meaning by habit and conditioning and do not continue to grow in your ability to know reality, then you have little control over the quality of your life.

You can't escape two facts: You are designed to find deeper meaning and knowing of reality, and you are driven to growth and evolution whether consciously or not. The truth is this: *Growth is a lot easier when it is done consciously.*

Your emotional state is determined by the meanings you assign. Your energetic state is determined by the meanings you assign. Your health ultimately is determined by the meanings you assign. This is the nature of life. You cannot fight your growth and evolution and your ability to assign ever greater and more accurate meanings. You are designed to grow and evolve your meanings and experience to know your true nature and the reality of life. Why? Because it is natural to grow. It is natural to seek greater freedom, happiness and joy, greater love and greater success. When have you heard someone say I want less happiness, less love, less money in my life? It is simply not natural. You are designed to grow and to come to know reality. And this reality is ultimately *nonmaterial*. Reality is energetic (or spiritual, if you will).

“

Growth is a lot easier when it is done consciously.

”

Even relationships are basically energetic. It is not so much the words, but the energy behind them. It is an oft-cited fact that only 7% of communication is verbal, and 93% is nonverbal. The energy that is carried in the tone, the inflexion, the body language, and the emotion behind the words all communicate much more than the words ever can. Change the tone or emphasis on words, and the entire meaning changes. Read these words emphasizing the words in capitals:

Did YOU see him take my towel?

Did you SEE him take my towel?

Very different meanings.

For you to assign the greatest, most uplifting and complete meaning requires you to grow to your full potential. For humanity to grow and begin to solve its many challenges, it is necessary for each of us to grow and understand there are ways to accelerate our growth. What remains to grow after you have reached age 20? On the physical level, the interconnections within the brain and the coherent functioning within the brain.

You will have a poor quality of life and a life full of challenges if you are only using part of your brain. You need to continue to make connections and *integrate* the functions of the nervous system. Ever experience that your mind says one thing, but your gut or heart says another? This is a lack of integration where you enter into conflict because of a lack of coherence and integration. "I know I should do it, but I don't want to." And so it goes, until you grow.

"

For you to assign the greatest, most uplifting and complete meaning requires you to grow to your full potential.

"

At the beginning of your development and growth your brain might look like the following. This is what a functional MRI scan of the brain might look like of someone who is not using their full potential and who demonstrates a high level of survival oriented behavior (habitual, fear-based, egoic behavior).

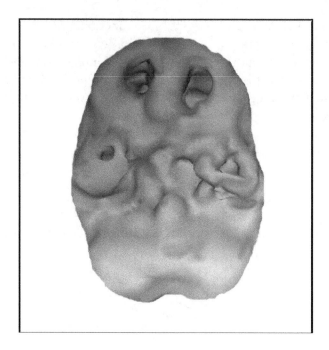

You see functional holes — areas of the brain that are not being used. As we develop more, our brains become more fully used like the following image.

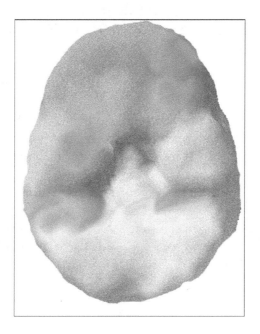

With fuller brain function you will have fuller experience and less internal conflict and contradiction, less survival-oriented behavior (less egoic behavior). You are more at peace with yourself.

This growth is what is natural, but it is not fostered, encouraged, accelerated or even recognized by most people. It is stunted in our culture. It is thwarted with distractions, drugs, alcohol, addictions, stress, loss of sleep — all elements that profoundly affect the brain and its integration. And so you go against your nature and thwart it. You often stop growing and never use your full potential. Psychologists in studying the brain long ago declared that you only use a small portion of the brain's capacity — 15-20% maximum. Now with functional MRI you can see this is not just an estimate — you can literally see parts of the brain not functioning, leaving "functional holes." The result? Violence, unmitigated selfishness, power mongering, greed, depression, anxiety, stress and illness. Just look at the maladies of our society, and you can begin to see the result of our not utilizing our full potential.

This is the most important transformation and the most needed element in society currently. It is the transformation that you need to take your life to a whole other level. This is what is needed to transform your health, wealth, happiness and success. This is your personal revolution — a revolution based on evolution.

The fact that your brain can function better — that your potential can be reached — is too often missed. The offer of a better brain doesn't fit with what most people think:

"Intelligence is inherited."

"You can't teach an old dog new tricks."

"This is just the way I am."

All of these expressions reflect a culture that does not recognize human growth or human potential. When the norm is to stunt growth, the assumption will be that nothing you do can change the brain or your intelligence.

This is the amazing awesomeness of modern times. You can easily have the knowledge, the techniques and the understanding of human potential. It is not just growing in knowledge — it is expanding the container of knowledge.

Your nervous system is the key to your life. It is the tool through which you perceive and assign meaning. Scramble it with a concussion, mess it up with drugs, damage it, and your ability to function, to have success, happiness, a quality life all go out the window. You will not be able to understand life, perceive properly, have good relationships or success in any tangible terms. You will lose your "spirit" or energy and assign meanings that create further problems and difficulties.

When you are able to develop yourself, you perceive reality and assign higher meanings until you are able to directly intuit, cognize or perceive the truth of life. This can literally save your life. The importance of meaning in life is the basis of an entire psychotherapy called *Logotherapy*. This was started by Victor Frankl based on his experiences in a German concentration camp during World War II. Frankl observed that those who could still find meaning in life within the concentration camp would survive much longer than those who could find no meaning. He began to see that meaning and purpose in life are essential to psychological health, and finding these often cures depression and other psychological disorders.

You get your *spirit* back when you find meaning and purpose in life. This is what began to happen to me that fortuitous day running in the rain. You come to know the deeper reality of life — that life is incredibly meaningful and that all is organized with exquisite intelligence. The "path" to finding this reality and the Ultimate Reality is a pathless path — one that you tread, not in miles but in inner growth.

This is for your mind's understanding. I understand your heart longs for ease in life. Your heart longs for love and connection. The mind convinces you that these are all unrelated. One is a head and the other a "tail-thingy." Your suffering, your struggles, your success and your happiness — they are all connected to your growth and your inner development.

Children develop by playing at life. Play is at once serious and fun. And such is the design for all of life unless you interfere with it and get away from what is natural. A child plays with toys and roles and has fun doing it when left alone.

When you aren't rested and aren't nourishing the growth of the nervous system, then it is hard to be clear on who you are and what is natural *for you*. The groundwork has not been laid. Like a child whose nervous system is not developed — thus they cannot perform algebra — you simply cannot realistically expect it. A fatigued and stressed adult nervous system limits opportunities for meaning and prevents expansion and growth from occurring.

Mastery involves inner growth. When you grow, your nervous system grows — your understanding of reality grows, your ability to intuit grows, your spirit grows, and your ability to love and to succeed grows. With all this your health grows.

Health comes from the word *Heilen,* meaning "to become whole." Our minds make a distinction between health, personal growth, spiritual development, spirituality and love, yet when you *become whole* you become healthy, you grow up, you develop spiritually, and you develop the nervous system to its full potential. These are not separate things. These are all the same — all interdependent and all from the same root.

It is time to understand how to live beyond your wildest imagination. It is time to start living the potential you never knew you had. And with this you will find the greatest love you have ever known.

"

It is time to understand how to live beyond your wildest imagination... And with this you will find the greatest love you have ever known.

"

Piaget's Story

What is the story of you? What wisdom will be written in your soul from this experience of life? The story of triumph or the story of tragedy? The story of the greatest love? The story of the noblest spirit? The hero's story? The story of the prodigal son?

What is the truth you have discovered through all your experiences? Story has gotten a derogatory meaning, referring to being lost in illusion and out of the present moment. But our souls have a history and come into this world with a past. Our experiences and the stories we tell ourselves about them make for the greatest learning. What is the story of you?

Is your story one of finding yourself or one of constantly being in conflict with yourself? Is your story one of self-sabotage, always coming close to success but never having it? Is your story one of heartache and loneliness? What has your experience been? What secrets have you discovered?

For many, it is yet to unfold. Unfold it will. It is the nature of life.

The story of your life is ultimately the story of love finding itself. But rather than telling you the end of the story, let me tell you more about the beginning and what your soul has been up to. The big secret is that your soul was up to something in each one of your experiences. They are not random. The hidden secret of life is not how to become a billionaire, win friends and influence people, or how to win the lottery or get early retirement. It is how we grow with each and every experience.

❝

The story of your life is ultimately the story of love finding itself.

❞

You are designed to grow in all ways: in knowledge, in intelligence, in spirit, in love, in success and in health and vibrancy. When you stray from what is natural you stop growing. For years I have studied and taught a system of medicine that is based on what is natural — Ayurveda. The primary cause of disease in this system is said to be *Pragya Aparadh* or being out of tune with our nature.

Your story is the story of life, which began a very long time ago. What you were never taught in school is how this life works. You were never taught how we grow and learn. And most important, you were never taught how to accelerate your growth.

The solution comes in growing the brain. How do you do that? Just like you grow a plant. *You* don't grow the plant. It is in its nature. You could say that nature grows the plant, not you. The same is true for you.

Your soul cannot live its story and experience what it came to experience if the vehicle that it is carrying it is not developed enough. If you were stuck in a five-year-old's body, you would have a hard time having the intelligence and clear perception of reality that would allow you to have experiences that contribute to your maturity, happiness and success.

So your story must be understood in terms of the soul and its purpose. That only becomes apparent when you use a majority of your potential. Up until that point, the soul is just going along for the ride. The undeveloped nervous system with its uncanny ability to misperceive reality dominates the story. You are attached to what others think about you, and you worry about money, status and prestige, and who likes whom. You miss the reality of who you are, how short life is and how the game of life is actually to be played. In other words, you miss what you came here to do as a soul.

You can't figure out what the soul came here to do until you develop yourself sufficiently. The game of life is actually about learning what is ultimately real and who you ultimately are and why you are experiencing what you are experiencing. "You can't get there from here" is a famous Maine saying. You can't get to the business of the soul until you have sufficiently developed yourself to not be dominated by the mind, the senses, the self-concept or the ego. To understand how to get there, learning how your interaction with reality is intimately tied to the nervous system is necessary.

Your growth comes with further development of the brain and the nervous system. It cannot be separated from that. When you have the framework of development from the standpoint of the brain, then you will understand how each element growth unfolds. You will understand the unfolding of consciousness. You will understand the essence of wisdom. So, my friend, without going into tons of boring research and at the risk of being criticized for oversimplifying the science of it all, let me explain the functioning of the brain and inner growth.

First of all, the brain specializes. It puts one set of functions in one half or one hemisphere of the brain. Typically, in the left hemisphere you have language function. All the talking to ourselves that we call thought (verbal thinking) is left brain. The ability to analyze and to use logic is all left brain. Most important, the sequential unfolding of time is left brain.

Language and time perception enable you to make concepts and interpretations of reality. You can interpret the past and from it predict the future. Also, significantly, your concept of yourself — your ego — is a left-brain function. All of the ego-programming and mental-emotional patterns have their roots in the left brain, because these are language-bound.

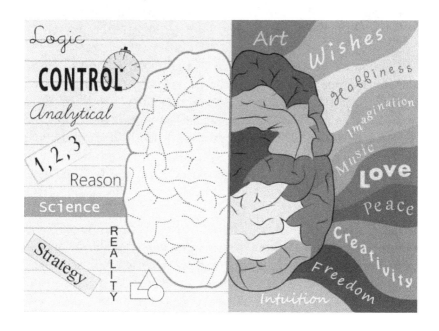

Compare this with the right brain. The right brain is timeless. There is only the present moment. It is silent except for the perception of music. It is where peace and love are experienced. It is where happiness and bliss are experienced. It is where creativity and imagination originate — where the ability to perceive form and patterns of energy reside and where the ability to form new patterns of energy come from. It is where the big picture and the holistic view reside.

Meditation plays a huge role in integrating the two sides of the brain. It is no mistake that the most efficient meditation practices emphasize the sound value of a mantra. In Heart-based Meditation the singing of the mantra is emphasized, as the sound carries one efficiently out of left-brain language and into the bliss of the present in the right brain. Through this, you come easily to the bliss of the heart. Once again, I am getting ahead of myself...

Meditation allows the dominance of the thinking mind to let go and inner peace and silence to be experienced. With this letting go, the restful alertness of the nervous system produces alpha brainwaves. Alpha waves are associated with great relaxation and peaceful alertness. At its most profound depth, this produces a coherency between the two hemispheres of the brain — a style of functioning that will develop outside of meditation after repeatedly experiencing it.

Imagine what this means in terms of day-to-day experience. In the midst of thinking, you have a relaxed restful alertness. You have an underlying happiness that gives a sense of presence and an ability to be in the now, while simultaneously planning and using logic to solve problems and look to the future. You know the reality of things. You see the big picture, and you keep things in context and at the same time see amazing detail and the patterns and connections in the details. You maintain a sense of peace in the midst of great mental and physical activity. You have the awareness to observe thoughts and to choose whether you will react to them or not. You are rarely triggered as a result.

You experience great love for life and people. You know the awesomeness of each moment, even in the midst of intense activity. Life takes on a very different quality and a richness that is indescribable.

This is the development that awaits you. In particular, coherence in the frontal lobes (the front part of the brain) is incredibly important. The frontal lobes are responsible for impulse control, the ability to delay gratification, good judgment, problem-solving ability, attention and memory. Your ability to attend, to be present, to use good judgment and delay gratification — your ability to be free from emotional triggers and to choose which emotional reactions you will run with — these come with increased frontal lobe coherence.

All of this means that a wonderful new life awaits you as you grow and develop yourself. This development requires meditation as a foundation.

Imagine life without this foundation. You can get a sense of this by imagining that you have the brain of a four-year-old. This is something brilliantly described by Jean Piaget, the father of the psychology of cognitive development. His work on the development of cognitive structures has influenced almost every area of psychology, from learning and cognition to child development and testing. The essence of his genius lies in a simple, yet profound recognition: It is not that a child is simply inexperienced and unlearned, rather that a child's brain is organized differently from an adult's. Children think and perceive reality differently from adults. It is the brain's functioning that makes for a different experience of life. The easiest way to describe this difference is to use one of his classic experiments:

> *Take a bowl that is fat, has a large radius, but is not very tall. Take a cylinder that is thin, has a small radius, and is tall. Then take a 6 oz. glass full of water and pour its contents in the fat bowl. Now refill the glass and pour it into the tall cylinder. Now look at both. Which has more?*

How you answer that question depends on the structure and functioning of the brain and how accurately that functioning allows for a true perception of reality. Most adults will clearly state that they have the same amount of water. Now ask most four-year-olds. Half of them will say that the bowl has more. If you ask them why, they will say, "It has more because it is fatter." The other half will say that the cylinder has more. If you ask them why, they will say, "It has more because it is taller." Now here is the important point. This is *reality* for them. It does not matter how often you explain to these children that the two appear to be different but are really the same. Seeing the same amount poured into each cylinder does not matter — experience and education do not matter. This is the child's reality — the child *knows* they are different.

You can bribe four-year-olds into giving you the correct answer by giving them some cookies or some other reward. But if you pull them aside and ask them what they really *believe*, they will tell you one or the other "really has more." They simply do not have the brain structure to be able to perceive in two dimensions. They can't take into account two variables — height and width. If you do the same experiment with eight-year-olds, you find that they give a very different answer. The vast majority of them will know that the contents of the two containers are equal. They can think in two dimensions, not because they are "smarter," rather because their brains have been wired through growth to perceive reality more fully.

Piaget made many such experiments and concluded that there are distinct stages in cognitive development. It did not matter what the I.Q. of the child was, how good his or her memory was, or how quickly they learned. Until a different style of functioning of the brain occurs, the ability to perceive more than one dimension of reality is simply not present. The four-year-old thinks in one dimension. His or her comprehension of reality is based entirely on information from the senses, and because the perception is undeveloped, it is one-dimensional. If the height dimension strikes the child as the most outstanding feature, then the cylinder has more. If the width dimension is predominant, then the bowl has more.

This is analogous to normal waking consciousness before the brain is developed — before the practice of meditation and the integration of the left and right brain are solid. Here your awareness of yourself is overshadowed by thoughts, emotions or physical sensations. You do not have that background of peace or holistic perception. You "identify" with one or more of these to the exclusion of your awareness of yourself as the observer of the thoughts, emotions or sensations. Until consciousness is more developed, fragmentation in the perception of reality is the norm.

Imagine what the world would be like if you and everyone else had the neurobiology of a four-year-old. Suppose everyone appeared grown physically to adulthood. Everyone could remember and learn things, so no one would know the difference. But when confronted with a dilemma like the one of which container has "more," what would happen?

Without an ability to *know* reality, there would be the development of various systems of beliefs. Most likely one set of beliefs would be formed by the "Tall-ists" and another by the "Wide-ists." Each would believe they knew what was real. They would have fervent arguments about why their beliefs were right and why it is important that others believe as they do. They would believe sincerely and strongly about their views and feel uncomfortable around those who held the opposite view. They might even get into fights about it. Worse yet, they might believe so strongly in their limited perception that they turn their beliefs into a religion and go on crusades trying to convert people to their way of believing, making others feel less worthy if they did not believe. In the most tragic case, they would wage war in the name of their beliefs, feeling it was their righteous duty.

Or, they would form political parties, each believing they had the best interest of the country at stake because they could see what was real, whereas the other party was obviously unrealistic. They simply see the other party as not knowing what is real and leading the country into the abyss.

Does this sound familiar? If it does, then you recognize that most of the world's challenges are the result of the underdevelopment of the human nervous system.

Suppose you go away and live in the Himalayas and develop the brain of an eight-year-old. You come back and look with curiosity at all the political and religious bickering and say, "No, no, no. There is no need for all of this. They are not different. They are all the same. It is the same water that goes into both. It is one and the same."

The four-year-olds would certainly be taken aback and say, "Are you crazy? Anyone can see they are different. Why would you ever believe this theoretical 'unity' garbage? It is just mystical mumbo-jumbo — just another unreal set of beliefs." The greater perception of reality becomes labeled and discounted as "mysticism," because it is a mystery to the four-year-old brain how anyone could perceive things as being the same.

Once you develop yourself, then the mysterious becomes commonplace reality. And what an awesome reality it is. Reality is described in mystical terms, but it is attained through development, not through belief. Ultimately, while opening to inner development requires faith and trust, it is actually by trusting and becoming innocent that we can let go and grow and develop ourselves.

Our current world is made up of four-year-olds when you look at the full development of the brain and the development of consciousness. There are a few "eight-year-olds" around, but they often don't know what they did to outgrow the rest of the population. This is where understanding the path of inner development and growth is crucial. It is this full human development that allows us to more accurately and more completely know reality. It is key to your growth and success in life.

Now that we have some of the technical details laid out, let me make the key elements clear, dear friend. You need two things to hasten your growth and development:

1) A method to expand awareness — meditation. Remember meditation means a lot of different things to different people, and the most effective meditations are those that use sound to go beyond the thinking mind and turn inward. Such techniques are Heart-based Meditation, Primordial Sound and Transcendental Meditation.

2) A system of methods to integrate this greater awareness into our left-brain patterning, so that you can be freed from the egoic programming and habits. This integration of awareness yields profound realizations about oneself, life and love.

There are two paths in spiritual development. These are often divided into a monk's path and a householder path. The distinction is blurred now that so many householders have adopted monk or ascetic type paths, emphasizing nonattachment and such. One emphasizes awareness up and out of the body. The other emphasizes integrating awareness into the body and into the life.

Those who suffer much in life want to escape and tend to want to go to the ashram and just sit in the expanded awareness of the monk's path. They spurn integrating the awareness into all areas of life. Those who come into life very evolved or developed often become attracted to integration techniques — be here now, be in the present, love what arises, love the inner child. But you need both. You need to have something to integrate. You need to have a method to integrate it. Some paths emphasize meditation and claim that that is all that needs to be done. Yet, you see highly evolved people, people who have sat at the feet of gurus behaving in unethical and immature ways. Meditation is fundamental. You must have the experience of being, the right-brain timelessness. You need this experience. And you need to integrate this experience and reprogram the thinking mind, the egoic patterns and programming that have been running (and usually ruining) the experience of life.

Along the way, if you adopt both, your growth will lead to new and profound realizations: The realization that you are never alone or the realization that you always are being watched over and guided, for example. These are transformative realizations. Each milestone, each shift transforms your life, your actions, your behavior and most important your heart. Each time you come to this deep knowing, life is different forever.

This is what I want most for you. The greatest realizations are those about love. As my greatest teacher has said, "Teach love." Yet, I am aware that what I teach has come *from the realizations born of the integration of greater awareness.* To have the information without true realization can be quite empty and worthless. The mind will want to argue or it will want to believe. I want you to *know.*

“

Information without true realization can be empty and worthless.

”

I will present these realizations because they can serve as previews of coming attractions. They can also serve you as you engage in your meditation practice to help you restructure the thinking mind, the emotional patterning and the energetic body. These three must be part of the integration process. I have presented the techniques for expanding awareness. I will present the technique for reprogramming with the further story of Jan. And later, the technique for working with the energetic body will become clear. For now let us work with the mind. Let me show you where we are headed — into the core of love and life.

For I want to help you to be in the perpetual experience of love. Being in the perpetual experience of love is being "in love" with or without a partner. Being in love is being in the experience of the fullness of your own heart. It goes way beyond romance. By "being in love" I mean being in the full experience of your heart and its capacity. When you are in love, you heal. When you are in love, you loosen the identification with the fear, the sorrow, the grief, the frustration and anger. When you love the emotion, you let it go and flow without getting lost in it. When you love what you are feel, you step back from it and let it flow. You acknowledge that you are separate from it and that "you" don't have to be consumed by it. You can choose to let it go. Being in this love is the key to emotional health, the key to evolving and to spiritual development. It is the key to happiness, and the key to heaven on earth.

Being in this love is what I long for — for me, for you, for all of humanity. When you are in this love, you are healing yourself and the world. Being in love is living in the fullness of love and light. When you live in the fullness of love and light, then you are happy. You are at peace. You find ease and grace.

Romantic love only opens you up to the possibility of the full heart. Because you have had no other way to experience the beauty of living unity with a full heart, you assume that being in love only comes with romance. It is said that we "fall" in love. What falls down? The ego. We let go completely into the heart. Sometimes this happens with the birth of a child. But usually the lack of equality in the relationship opens the heart while affecting the ego in a different way.

Be in love. Sit in the fullness of your wonderful and tender heart. This is what I long for, for you and for all of humanity. How do you get there? It is not a matter of will. It is not a matter of belief. It is not a matter of understanding or insight. It is the result of inner growth, human growth — the growth we were designed for as adults — adult human development.

❝

When you live in the fullness of love, then you are happy.

❞

More Jan

Jan was instrumental in my understanding of integration techniques. She was brilliant in her wisdom and the clarity and authenticity with which she presented things. And she was no nonsense, often blunt and lovingly confrontational. The first technique she taught me was affirmations. She explained these in ways I had neither heard nor read. She explained how the subconscious mind is always listening, how consciousness is creative, not just passive, and how we tell ourselves things all day long, sometimes clearly and sometimes subtley.

If you tell yourself that you are not good enough, that there you go again doing it wrong, that you need to hide yourself, you integrate this and it becomes programmed in the subconscious mind. In order to reprogram the subconscious mind, we must recognize two things. First, it takes thousands of repetitions of the new program, not just a few here or there, to counter the old. Jan said she used to jog for 35 minutes each day and she used this time to repeat her affirmations. This way she would get in hundreds of repetitions each day. Second, the intensity of emotion behind the words is important. Without intensity the subconscious mind takes longer to "hear" the message and start the reprogramming process.

Jan helped me internally reprogram who I was and how I was to change the world. For many years my challenge had been to find a way to accept the suffering in the world and the blindness and corruption that seemed to perpetuate it. She explained how my attitude about the world was self-sabotaging. "If you see the world as imperfect, then you will be fighting against it. Who are you fighting against? God. Yourself. You are the world." This was a bit of a shock to say the least. By that time I had read enough about eastern philosophy and had experienced enough expansiveness in meditation to understand intellectually what she was trying to say. But my heart didn't get it. She saw that immediately and said, "You have learned and absorbed that the universe is one and that everything and everyone you see is part of the one. And if I say that I am God — part of the one — your mind will have no problem with it. But if I say that you are God, your mind won't get that. If you are part of the one, and you say the world is bad, then you undermine your energy, and you set yourself up for failure and frustration. You have to understand that the world is perfect." I looked at her with puzzlement. "How can you say that?"

"I can say that, because it is," she said.

I shook my head.

"Here. Look at these carnations that you brought me. What do you see?" My mind scrambled thinking this was some sort of test. They were just flowers. As if reading my mind, she said, "You see flowers, and your mind says 'beautiful flowers.' This is the way God sees everything. You innocently see the flowers. You don't start analyzing the flowers and looking at which one is better and how this one needs this or that. You see the beauty, and you say to yourself 'beautiful flowers.' But look at this bud. It isn't really a flower yet. Your mind doesn't say, 'This is terrible — such a bad flower. How disgusting. I have to do something about this.' No, you would never think that way.

The same is true with the world. There are people who are just buds and have much growing to do. That is perfect and as it is designed to be. Sure you can say 'I want to help these people grow.' But that has a much different energy and attitude than saying they are imperfect and need to be corrected. Even someone like Hitler is a bud that will eventually grow as a soul and come to something more than what he is known for. Each of us is designed to grow, but like each bud, we are perfect just as we are. You may prefer the full bloom of the flowers. I actually get more excited about the buds and the anticipation of how and when they will unfold. I get excited about the beauty that will unfold. Like that the world is unfolding. It is perfect in every way and will unfold even greater perfection. You can be a part of that, if you wish, but not if you attack it and get angry at it. Because it is who you ultimately are. You are the Universe."

Of course my mind was just spinning with this. I had spent so much time and energy seeing the world as imperfect and needing fixing that this was like speaking a foreign language. Still, a part of me recognized immediately the wisdom and the truth of this. Jan recommended I start programming the truth with affirmations. "I am God," was one. "I see perfection in all things," was one I also adopted. "I am releasing any thing, thought, habit, belief or person that is no longer part of the Divine plan for my life and am embracing all the wonderful new the Divine has for me," was another she recommended to let go of my old emotional and mental habits and ways of fighting with the world. It was profound. I only regret that I got off course and didn't continue this reprogramming until a time later. And that is perfect too.

＂

Each of us is designed to grow, but just like a flower bud, each of us is just perfect as we are.

＂

Where We Are So Far

Your growth and your development as an adult can be accelerated with effortless mantra-based (sound-based) meditation to expand awareness. This greater awareness needs to become part of your functioning. Integration of this greater awareness into your mind, emotions and energy is required. This includes restructuring your thinking and perspectives, your emotional reactions and the energetic flows that tend to hold emotions in place in your musculature and in the body. The mind can be reprogrammed with affirmations, particularly "I am" affirmations, as these restructure the reality of who you are and carry great power.

Emotions can be restructured through becoming mindful of triggers and by choosing a different reaction. Even more powerful is to become aware of the basic human needs that are running the programs and feeding the triggers. (More on that later when I go into Tony.) What you will discover is that a connection exists between human needs, emotions and what are called the chakras or energy centers in the body. When you reprogram these, profound transformations take place. You can facilitate this restructuring with energy work, the most profound of which is in the yoga tradition — especially Healing Light Yoga (www.healinglightyoga.com).

It is important to realize in all of this that the age of gurus is over. Teachers and guides will still be found, but the need for an exclusive tradition and reliance on the protection of a guru is coming to an end. As you develop your own internal guidance system, you will find the guru within. With that your growth will be accelerated and assured.

As you grow and develop, you will have many realizations. The word "realization" is very appropriate, as you will come to know what is real. I am presenting some of the realizations that have transformed my world, so you can know the power of this inner development. Do not "believe" any of them. I don't want you to adopt these and make them your perspective. No one needs another religion, even if it is a New Age religion. I offer them as coming attractions and with the knowledge that you might already be meditating and ready for these. The hope is that you will learn to think with the heart (the inner guidance system) and love with the mind. For the mind to become loving, significant restructuring of programming and perspective is needed. This takes place when you come to realization and know the truth.

This second section is more about the realizations and offers some methods of integration as well. May you be inspired, and may they serve you well.

"

As you develop your internal guidance system, you will find the guru within.

"

Part 2

The Realizations - Loving with the Mind

Judgment

"I have decided to stick with love. Hate is too great a burden to bear."
- Martin Luther King, Jr.

Mr. Tyler was my sixth grade teacher. He was from Tennessee and had a bit of an accent, which made him stand out from the rest of the Michigan teachers. He was in his mid-40s and could be very strict with his students, which did not win him any favors. He also had the habit of picking his nose. This earned him the height of all disfavor with us budding teenagers. I remember distinctly offering up my distaste for this teacher to my elder brother. He suggested that it didn't matter. "You can still learn a lot in spite of that." I was not persuaded. An adult who picked his nose just lost all respect in my mind. I felt he should know better.

Judgment works this way, my friend. You say, "This is not me. I would *never* do that." Why not? Because we are afraid of being that way. What are the inner workings of judgment? Here is the truth you never were told: What you judge, you become. It is one thing to discriminate this from that and say, "I prefer not to be that way." It is another to judge and say someone is bad. From the broadest of views that is saying God screwed up and created bad things. You may not like things — you may not want to promote or encourage them — but that is very different from saying they are bad and wrong. Judgment creates an emotional energy that binds you to what is judged. That's the inside secret. This energy becomes part of your energy system and creates a binding influence. Why? Because consciousness is creative. You begin to create that which you resist, because the more energy and attention you pour into it, the more you create it. Did you ever walk up and down a flight of stairs and then all of a sudden have the thought, "Oh, I better be careful. I might trip?" Then, as soon as you have the thought, you stumble? What you project energetically, you create.

When I got into my late 30s this weird thing happened to me — nose hair. I started noticing that it felt constantly like I had something in my nose. I felt compelled to check and make sure. Then I realized. This is what Mr. Tyler was doing. "Oh, my gosh," it humbled me. I had become what I had judged. Judgments work that way. I judge what I do not want to see in myself, either as reality or potentiality. I am blind to this potential in myself, because I make my self-judgment unconscious and hide from it. I hide from the small ways in which I imitate the big things I judge. I fear seeing that dark part of me — that shadow side of me.

Here is the inside scoop: What you fear, you pour energy into. And what you resist, persists. My mother often felt judgmental toward those who were not as smart as she was. She would use expressions like "that dumb old witch" and such. I later realized she was afraid of this shortcoming in herself. She placed a high value on education and on learning and worked very hard to put her sons through college and to pursue further studies herself. She feared being uneducated and "stupid." Out of that fear, she would judge others. It works that way. Now I am not saying that my mother created her Alzheimer's with this unconscious fear, but it was a bitter irony that this woman who valued education and intelligence so much would lose her faculties to Alzheimer's disease.

What you fear, you resonate with and, through the power of consciousness, you often become it. It is really not ours to judge, because the world is the Divine's. It is perfect in its unfoldment.

It is perfect that you want greater perfection to unfold — still, it is perfect as it is. When you judge, you say, "God, you screwed up." Here is the kicker: Since you are part of that whole, you are judging yourself. You are trying to create distance from the shadow side of yourself. You try to separate from what you ultimately fear. My mother was very afraid of "not being smart." Out of her fear, she came to judge.

The mind does this. It separates things and makes distinctions and rationalizes behavior. It is a terrible master. It tortures. It makes up stories to avoid the fear it creates. It runs and rushes from one thing to another. It creates a line of thinking that becomes mistaken for reality. Someone cuts you off on the highway, and the mind says how horrible they are and how they are so rude and out to get you and out to get ahead of everyone else. It rationalizes that it is your right and duty to give them the finger and pound on your horn. It gets your adrenaline pumping and your righteous indignation inflamed. It causes stress hormones to careen through your blood and strain your body — even damage it.

The mind replays the injustice over and over again. The mind has taken control of you. It has become your master. You are no longer free, and your body is paying the price. The mind is not aware of reality in that moment. If you could see the full picture, you would realize that that person might be having a heart attack. They might have almost passed out, or they might be rushing to get to a hospital. There may be a hundred other explanations that would cause you to be embarrassed to have judged them so harshly.

Even if it were something not so drastic, aggressive and hostile acts are born of pain — the pain deep within the individual motivates them to try to control the external environment. The more severe the pain, the deeper the wounds, the more suppressed the awareness of them, the greater the aggressive, self-centered behavior and the need for control. This is what the mind does. But because it does not want to look at itself, facing the pain and what it is doing, the person ends up with no choice but to be angry. *You* have a miserable day because someone has cut you off on the highway today. *You* suffer, not the person on the highway.

The mind is a wonderful tool and a horrible master. Our path to freedom is to learn to think with the heart and love with the mind. This is where real inner freedom and liberation reside. Loving with the mind doesn't mean you chastise yourself every time you catch yourself judging. This is just another expression of judgment itself. Loving with the mind comes in creating compassion and self-forgiveness for yourself and others that paves the way to inner peace and true tolerance. When you forgive yourself for the times you have been aggressive with others, when you can find true self-compassion, then you pave the way to finding compassion with others.

‹‹

Our path to freedom is to learn to think with the heart and love with the mind.

››

Just read the following words out loud. It doesn't work to just read them silently to yourself. Read them out loud and feel into them. Then notice what happens.

I forgive myself for judging others.

I forgive myself for judging myself.

I forgive myself for being rude to others.

I forgive myself for the ways I have ignored others' needs.

I forgive myself for the ways I have ignored my own needs.

I forgive myself for the ways I have let others down.

I forgive myself for the pain I have tried to cover up.

I forgive myself for not having compassion for the pain I carry.

I forgive myself for being afraid of the world.

I forgive myself for being afraid of others' aggressiveness and not seeing it as an expression of their pain.

I forgive myself for being afraid.

I forgive myself for thinking I am so different from others.

I forgive myself for not loving all that I am.

I forgive myself for not accepting and loving those painful parts of myself.

I forgive myself for the pain.

I forgive.

I forgive.

With this practice of self-forgiveness you attain to peace. You begin to transform the mind and shift it to its proper function of being a tool for love. Judgment heralds that place within us that needs healing. It heralds the place that holds fear and ultimately self-judgment. It heralds where we need to focus for our further growth. Let each judgment uncover the hidden fears and pains so that you can bring them into the light — so that love can heal them and bring you to true inner peace. Each time you find yourself judging, practice self-forgiveness. Self-compassion and self-forgiveness are the gateways to inner freedom. These transform the critical, judgmental tyranny of the mind to the capacity to love with the mind and to leave the thinking and deciding to the heart. Use this tool and be blessed with love and inner freedom.

Happiness & Expectations

How often has my mind been my undoing? How often have I created great unhappiness with my expectations of how things "should" be? So much of my adolescence was unhappy because of my awareness of the world and how it did not make sense or fit my expectations. It was important and is important to recognize the entirety of the world — good and bad. But doing so developed habits in the mind of cynicism and criticalness, which did not serve me.

Ultimately, happiness comes from within you. Ultimately, it is a reflection of the heart finding the freedom to be in its open, expansive, awe-filled, loving space. The mind learns, almost like Pavlov's dog, that when I get what I want, it feels good. The ultimate truth is that when a goal is reached or a desire is fulfilled, then you unlock the potential fulfillment that is in the heart. As you grow and develop this is one of the hallmarks of inner growth — the realization that happiness is not dependent on something or someone outside of you. One of the greatest illusions that robs all of humankind is that something outside of you will make you happy. This illusion puts people at odds with each other, fighting for what they desperately seek and hold as the key to happiness. This can be money, a job, a family, a home or a million other things. The happiness is not outside — it is inside. The mind triggers a release of the goal. The goal has been met. The conditions for happiness have been met. There is a relaxation and a letting go that occur. In that moment of letting go, then you come to experience what is deep within you. You feel satisfied. But you do not reside in this for long. The mind carries you away and then begins to seek another goal, follow another desire, and off you go.

The mind stands in the way of happiness with its endless seeking for something more. This is not wrong. This is the way you are designed. You are also designed to grow and to discover through this growth that what you seek is already within you. Even enlightenment. I have heard many enlightened sages say that enlightenment is an uncovering of what is already there — that you are already enlightened — that you just need to wake up to it.

In the process of growing your base of awareness and your awareness of the bliss of life, your integration and experience will be greatly enhanced by understanding expectations and the nature of happiness.

"

What you seek is already within you.

"

I have tremendous respect for Tony Robbins. And he has much to say about happiness and expectations. He explains that, for most of us, happiness comes when our expectations or idea or map of the world match the way our life actually is. A mismatch between what we want or expect and what actually is creates unhappiness. His recommendation is that you choose to change your map — change your expectations — or change your life. And for most of us this is an appropriate and beneficial way to deal with expectations and happiness.

However, for those who are interested in growing and in maximum growth there is a third option. This third option is finding happiness in being — building a reservoir of happiness within. It is in the fullness of the heart, in the radiance of innocent being, perceiving the fundamental awesomeness of the moment that you attain to the happiness that goes beyond the mind. Leave the mind, and enter into the realm of the heart. You shift from mental expectations and fulfillment of goals and desires to a state of pure being in which the experience of love, peace and bliss fill your existence. They persist in the background regardless of the mind's conjurings.

Borrowing an analogy from the great spiritual teacher Maharishi Mahesh Yogi serves here. He talks about the man who is walking down the street and gets his wallet stolen. If that man is homeless and is without a job, the wallet represents the last money that he has. This creates tremendous stress, suffering and unhappiness. If, on the other hand, the man is a billionaire, it is still unfortunate, but creates very little stress. It is more of an inconvenience. It does not impact his happiness. He just goes to the bank and gets some more money and more credit cards and goes on with his day. It is the same event. It is the same situation. What is the difference? The difference is that the one man has much more in terms of resources and reserves.

When your heart is full, when you have an inner reserve of happiness, when you are anchored in the bliss and awesomeness of life, then you become like the billionaire. Expectations don't need to be met for happiness to result. The billionaire isn't happy that his wallet was stolen. Yet, his inner state is unaffected by it.

It is like when you fall in love. All the world is aglow with wonderment. You feel excited, and it really doesn't matter what happens, as long as you can spend time with your beloved. It is exactly like this, except there is no external lover. There is only life and the bliss of your own heart. Everyone becomes your beloved, as does life itself.

A lot needs to be cleared in terms of associations and expectations before this bliss comes to the forefront. You must build the foundation with meditation. You hasten the process by working with expectations consciously and cultivating the bliss of the heart.

❝

There is only life and the bliss of your own heart, and everyone becomes your beloved, as does life itself.

❞

I remember when I was in college and my girlfriend went away for a semester. I tried to visit her on the weekends. On the second weekend she was busy, and I had to wait another weekend. My brother happened to be in town, and she wanted to meet him, so he drove with me to the institute at which she was staying. My expectation was that we would visit for a bit and get something to eat and then she and I would have some alone time. My girlfriend was fascinated with my brother and wanted to keep talking with him after dinner and right up until bedtime. Then the kicker came when we went to bed, and she was too tired to make love. I was miserable. It had been two weeks since we had seen each other, and I had been so looking forward to it. I had great expectations to say the least.

Had I had more reserve in terms of my own inner happiness, I would have been able to roll with this and recognize that my girlfriend really wanted to get to know my family (a good thing and a good sign early in a relationship). I could have recognized that she would have been much more interested in making love after she was well rested. I could have recognized that she would have been better able to connect and share in the morning. But I didn't. I felt miserable, and I felt I needed to find out what was going on, and of course the results were predictable.

When you look to others for your happiness and when you have little awareness and reserve of bliss in the heart, then chasing after what you want and trying to control getting what you want makes life incredibly complicated. Of course my girlfriend and I had a terrible argument. She was tired. I was frustrated. We weren't connecting, and things spiraled out of control.

Having happiness reserve — having bliss in the heart as the basic foundation of your life — allows you to let go of expectations. Understand the structure of your expectations. It is often silent. It can be second nature to you. It can be something that is just there in the background. For some it might be that you expect to make more money this year than you did last year. "That is a sign of progress. It is a reasonable measure of success," you tell yourself. These expectations seem normal, natural, reasonable…

Tony Robbins tells the story of a financial expert who predicted the stock market crash of 2008. That year he made $650 million. The following year he was depressed. He only made $350 million, and his rule for happiness (his expectation) was that he must make *more* money each year than he did the previous year. I am sure that you would not be depressed if you made $350 million in the last year. You would rejoice. What seems reasonable — that to feel successful I have to make more money this year than last — is clearly unreasonable.

The key to loving with the mind is to restructure the wiring that insists that in order to be happy life must unfold exactly as you want it to. Remember the story of my ride not coming to pick me up and everything going wrong? In spite of that I had the experience of an exhilarating happiness. Life becomes much freer and easier when you stop insisting the entire universe conform to your standards and expectations and you begin to open to what is. Within "what is" you will find many exhilarating and inspiring things. The mind is facile. It can shift in an instant. Loving with the mind means not resisting what is. It is expecting the unexpected. It is understanding that "life is what happens while we are busy making other plans," to quote John Lennon.

For example, take a job loss — that is what is. Loving with the mind first means accepting that. It means coming to "this," knowing that it is the springboard for the next adventure in life. What will happen next? You now have an opening to many other opportunities and possibilities. You grieve the loss, but you don't hang on and insist that life be different than it is. You let your mind love the possibilities that have now opened.

You do not need to wish for or hope for less in life. You actually are well-served with aiming for and hoping for more. Loving with the mind means that you have faith that life will deliver to you exactly what you came here to experience. In that faith, you hope for and wish for much in life. You do so without expecting or demanding that life and the Universe become exactly how we want them to be. You love what is, knowing that it is what your soul has come here to experience.

Loving with the mind starts with acceptance. It is letting go of resistance and being able to flow, as the ups and downs of life come and go. It is having a background of stability and knowingness that all is and will be well. It is the invincibility of living from the depths of the heart. This originates from faith and its workings. This is where Aureya Magdalen helped me tremendously.

"

Loving with the mind means that you have faith that life will deliver to you exactly what you came here to experience.

"

Aureya - Your Soul's Permission

You can't let go of expectations without cultivating the quality of faith. The mind will run away with itself if it does not have this underlying stability and knowledge. Faith is not an irrational belief in something mysterious; rather, faith is confidence in the unknown. When we know with certainty that the Divine has organized life in a higher and perfect order, then we have confidence in the unknown. It is the confidence in knowing the flow of the unseen and inner workings of life. Belief is an insistence that the unknown is known. Faith is openness to the unknown that says, "I am confident it will all be okay." Faith is saying, "I trust the Universe to bring me exactly what I need to experience."

This quality of faith is a knowing that all will be okay — it is not a knowing of what will come. Many who focus on belief have certainty. They have followed the tenets of their religion and believe that only good things will come. They then have a crisis of "faith" when life presents something bad. True faith brings a confidence that you are exactly where you need to be and that nothing can happen to you without your soul's permission.

❝

True faith brings a confidence that you are exactly where you need to be and that nothing can happen to you without your soul's permission.

❞

This was a challenge for me to learn. My teacher, Aureya, would have compassion for what I was experiencing, but then would also ask me to see the reality. Suffice it to say, it took awhile. As the expression goes, "None is so blind as he who will not see."

Aureya explained, "Nothing happens to any of us without our soul's permission. In fact, on the level of the soul, the babies dying of AIDS in Africa are rejoicing." That is where I could not make the shift. How could an innocent child be joyous that they were dying of AIDS? I understood the part that our Higher Self was a part of the Divine. I understood that only with the Divine's permission could anything happen to you. It took a while to get to that point and to really understand how that works. I had seen enough soul contracts between individuals to know that people arrange for many types of experiences, some of them unpleasant, so that they can learn and can resolve old karma.

The first hurdle I was able to overcome was when I stopped seeing the Higher Self as this little ray of light connecting me to the heavens. It was not a tiny sliver of my existence. I began to see that what I normally identified with as my existence was just a sliver in my Higher Self. The soul and the Higher Self are huge, and the ego is tiny. I had to admit that if the soul and the Higher Self were part of the Divine, then being part of the Almighty, they could stop anything from happening that was not in the design of my life. It took a long time. But I finally was able to understand. However, little children being joyful about dying from a debilitating disease — that seemed nuts to me.

It did not change until I really looked hard at myself and the reality of what I had been experiencing. I understood that the soul arranges with other souls to meet and to learn or work through karma. This was clear in relationships. It was clear that people often have known each other in past lifetimes. It was clear their meeting wasn't circumstance. It was clear that their struggles were part of their learning. It made sense that they would arrange with one another to play these roles. So I was used to this aspect of the soul arranging things. It did make sense with what I was beginning to experience and see in remembering my own past lives. But this idea of rejoicing in suffering made no sense to me until I realized that it was my own judgment.

I pondered. "If karma is a debt, and they are paying back the debt, then maybe on a soul level they are glad to be done with the debt." Then it hit me. It was like paying off a mortgage. I knew what a relief it was to have a mortgage paid off — to no longer carry the burden of that responsibility. What if someone had tried to stop me from paying off my mortgage? "Oh, no, you are going to give all your money to the bank. Then you won't have it. Don't do it." If someone had approached me that way, I would have thought *they* were nuts. It was then that I realized Aureya was right. The soul rejoices to have the debt paid off. Dying as a young child is a fast way to burn up a lot of karma and pay back the debt.

That doesn't mean I shouldn't do anything to help dying children. That is my soul's job and purpose. But when I can't help, I accept what is and understand what is actually happening. If their soul did not give permission, it would not happen — someone would save the child.

Paying off the debt, the soul is relieved and rejoices. This is the realization that makes for one of the most profound shifts as you develop yourself: *You are 100 percent responsible for whatever happens to you.* There are no victims.

It takes time to come to this. It took me developing my own clairvoyance and helping many others with their past lives and their life lessons to get this. It took time to come to the point where this went from logic and theory to truth and reality. I present it to you to introduce what every soul comes to realize on its path of growth — that you, on the soul level, create your life. No one else is responsible except you.

This radical realization shifts the approach and the response to all of life with a dramatic release of all victim stories and patterns. It frees one to rapidly learn what the soul came here to learn and become truly free. It frees one to truly love and to live with boldness and clarity. This freedom is based on faith. It is based on knowing the truth of life. It is based on knowing that all is perfect with life and that you will be okay, regardless of what happens. More important, it is coming to know in your heart that love is always present and available to you. Loving life, loving yourself, loving the world — these carry you forward and make you free.

Love is the way, my friend. It is the key to integration. It is the key to growth. Love is not a sentiment, or an emotion, or a sensitive, tender concept. Love is forceful and powerful. It frees us and takes expanded awareness and turns it into bliss, joy and awesome ecstasy at each moment of your life. Love is the way.

To travel the path of love, you need a deeper understanding of love. What are its components? What are its subtle expressions? What is the masculine versus feminine expression of love? What is the way in which we create a habit with in the mind of seeing with love, of utilizing love, of thinking from the standpoint of love? How do we change the divisive, critical, analytical mind to become loving? How do we cultivate love? What is the source, course and goal of love?

Love is the way. To think with the heart, love what is present and use the mind to appreciate the details. To understand this, love must be explored in depth.

Love

"Love many things, for therein lies the true strength, and whosoever loves much performs much, and can accomplish much, and what is done in love is done well."
— Vincent van Gogh

"The best and most beautiful things in this world cannot be seen or even heard, but must be felt with the heart."
— Helen Keller

Heaven is here, now. My friend, you have within you treasures just waiting to unfold. You are to know that at any point on your path this is available to you: infinite love, pure joy. You may be in disbelief. As much as your mind does not want to believe, your heart knows. Deep beyond any notion of personal hurt, pain or grief, something more is present. At the core of every emotion, of every desire, of every aspect of life, even the consciousness that gives awareness — at the core of life and of all creation is love. The heart has the potential to expand and experience the infinite, to touch the Divine and to be in untold bliss.

Find a window to this place. It is your destiny to come to know this love. This may sound fanciful, unfathomable. Perhaps in the bliss of falling in love you have had hints of the treasure within. Maybe this occurred with the birth of a child, or in the depths of true friendship, a precious reunion with an old friend that touched and expanded your heart in an unexpected way. These events only scratch the surface of the potential of the heart. Love is your destiny because when you grow to know reality, this truth becomes clear. Love is the source of everything in creation. It is your essence. You cannot know reality and not know who you are in essence. Love is your essence. Love is who you are.

Love expresses itself in joy. Love and joy are one. Joy goes even beyond happiness. When you experience love and joy, you celebrate life and celebrate being. When you celebrate love, you find joy and cherish life. And when you honor joy, you find love and presence in living.

When you discover this, and when you integrate that discovery, then each moment affords an opportunity to come to love. Each moment can be a falling in love or, more appropriately, a soaring in love. It raises the entire life to an experience of awesome bliss. Each moment affords an opportunity to experience this. Every aspect of daily life brings the opportunity for this rising up, this soaring forth. This is not forced. It becomes the experience with the integration of growth, with the loving mind. Listen to a song, and its beauty can take you there. Shake a friend's hand, and you are reminded of the awesomeness of friendship, and you raise up. Look out your window and see the sun's vibrant colors reflecting off of everything, and the beauty and the unfathomable organization of life on earth around this sun will bring you to love, appreciation and bliss. This is the result of growth and development.

I have experienced how unfathomable this is. I have experienced thinking these sorts of words were unrealistic and impractical. I remember being cynical about the spiritual experience and later having to eat my words. I remember how incredibly low I set the bar for what was possible in life and having been shaken to the core to think at one point I questioned whether I wanted to live.

I remember when I had been doing some intense meditation courses and felt energy rise up my spine, exploding in waves of bliss — ecstasy beyond even the most intense sexual experience. I was working in a psych ward, and the team was discussing what to do for a depressed patient. The discussion focused on the importance of sex. I mentioned there were more important things. "Name me one thing that is more pleasurable," challenged one of the nurses in response. I was ready to name three, but I knew that my experience was so far out of the ordinary that no one would be able to connect with it, let alone believe me. I remembered how cynical I had been when hearing descriptions of spiritual and religious experiences. My friend, you have no idea what awaits you when you cultivate full growth. Once you experience the ecstasy of infinite love, my friend, you will never forget. And you will seek this until it is permanent.

The potential your heart has is beyond amazing. You get little glimpses of this when you fall in love or are moved by music or by friendship. But these are just glimpses. Let me give you a way to understand these words. When you reach silence in meditation, the entire brain becomes synchronized, and the stimulation of one part of the brain stimulates all parts. Energy rising up can open the heart and *anything* that evokes love brings ecstatic bliss. Sounds can have colors or feel to them. Colors can shimmer with light that seems translucent. That is why the ancient sages called the silent, pure consciousness *Sat Chit Ananda. Sat* means "pure." *Chit* means "consciousness." And *Ananda* means "bliss." This is the reality of life — it is utterly amazing, beyond belief.

The essential core of your existence is love, and it expresses the bliss of being. Not a bliss that is peaceful, although it often starts that way. In meditation you may find a break from the pain, pressure and suffering, and it can be such a relief that you perceive that peace as blissful. That is just the beginning. The full story is that that peace and bliss eventually become rich with an awe-provoking ecstatic blissfulness that is, in essence, love. Opening the heart is required. Living in the heart is the way to cultivating the full potential for all bliss and ecstasy.

Opening the window to the heart can be like peeling back the layers like peeling an onion. This is the work of integration. I will give you some layers in the following pages. But every and any aspect of love can bring us to the full experience of its ecstatic potential. Whether it is forgiveness or gratitude or acceptance or compassion or caring or kindness or generosity or appreciation or protecting and providing — every shade of love can be a window to the core of our being — love supreme. Find that way into the heart, use it, and your life will transform.

The path can be long and winding, or it can be short and instantaneous. Come to the core of your being, to the true heart, by whatever path you may, and discover the awesome power and ecstasy of pure love. Peel back the layers of anything that stands in the way. This is what integration means. This is the way to the loving mind and living in the heart. For we cannot find a way out of suffering until we find a pathway to the true heart.

Love is tender, it is kind, it is nurturing. These qualities are so lacking in our culture that you may find yourself drawn to them. You may have not had this growing up as a child. So many of us didn't. Or maybe your parents only loved *their* projection of who you were. Love like this falls short and does not nourish. The result is a pull toward an honoring of the Divine Feminine and the nurturing aspects of love. This is so apparent in much of the New Age culture. Just as many are drawn to resurrect the Divine Feminine to restore the nurturing, kind, tender aspects of love and compassion, the understanding of masculine love and its importance in promoting feminine love is lost.

Masculine love is protective, caring, powerful and dynamic. The father that protects his family, the neighbor who comes to your aid, the friend who cares and shows it through acts and deeds, the parent who provides for the family — these are all expressions of masculine love. Masculine love holds space for the feminine. You have felt masculine love if you have ever felt someone being truly present with you, fully attentive, fully caring and allowing you to express what is on your mind and in your heart.

One of my business mentors describes an incredibly expensive business coach who does not do phone or Internet consults. You have to travel to his home to meet with him in addition to the thousands you spend to have access to his coaching. This man has a flagpole outside his house, and he creates a flag specifically for you, which flies on the day of your arrival. He spends a great deal of time preparing himself to meet with you. He meditates and intuits what is needed and expresses this intuition in the design of the flag. He wakes up early on the day he is to meet with you, and he has a ritual that he performs to prepare himself to be fully present when you meet. And presence is what you feel. Almost everyone who works with him comments on how heard and understood they feel after they meet with him. Many express how they feel really heard for the first time in their lives. This is not a business coaching technique. This is being fully present and caring deeply about what is being said. This is masculine love.

Presence, attentiveness, protection, caring, dynamic action born of love, acts of love and the explosive ecstasy of love — these are the masculine expressions of love. The rush of ecstatic love I experience in meditation and its incredible power, going far beyond even sexual pleasures — this is the masculine expression of love. This is love worth seeking.

Don't be deceived, my friend, by the words masculine and feminine. Every human being has both. While we may favor one side or the other, we have both aspects of love in our hearts and both types of energy in our beings. When you marry the masculine presence, power and protection of love with the nurturing, kind, generous, tenderhearted, vulnerable, feminine love, then the full power of love is born. In the entire universe nothing is more powerful.

I learned the martial art of Aikido. The founder of this art was still alive when I was born. He was quite old in the 1960s, but there were many films of him throwing attackers around like ragdolls on the demonstration mat. He had been in the military, fighting the Chinese, at a time when guns were a rare commodity. Much of the fighting was done by sword. He tells the story of being surprised by an army of 300 Chinese. He fought them off single-handedly and after three hours of fighting, none of the Chinese could get past his expert skill with the sword. Not wanting to risk any more losses, they withdrew, realizing none of them had the skill to harm or kill this man. Still, as powerful and proficient a warrior as he was, the thing that many of his students commented on was this: He could look a tough man in the eye with such presence and love that the man would start to cry and lay down his weapons.

I have had experience with the power of this presence. Through a great gift I was given the opportunity to look a man in the eyes during a workshop and say nothing. As I did this, I felt the presence of the angelic with me and poured the love from my eyes into his. A very masculine, former rugby player, his eyes began to tear up and he started to weep without me saying a word. This is pure presence. This is masculine love.

The marriage of the feminine and masculine creates a power unsurpassed by any power in the universe. It creates a power that can draw two souls together from the ends of the earth. It is a power that transforms lives. It is a power that heals all. It is the power of the Universe made manifest.

This is the power that awaits you. You can come to it through releasing the programming and patterns that you have learned in the past. Releasing the old ways of getting love, the old ways of thinking and emoting, can bring you to the pure essence of the heart. Or you can go directly there through any one of love's qualities. Take gratitude, and make it your constant habit, and you will find your way to the full power of love. Or take acceptance, and come to complete and total surrender, and acceptance of that comes to your awareness. You can come to it this way. Or your soul may be calling out to learn all the aspects of feminine and masculine love. You may come to it by peeling away the layers of illusion and coming to know your true, core self — a pure heart that holds all power and all vulnerability simultaneously.

"

We cannot find a way out of suffering until we find a pathway to the true heart.

"

My friend, you cannot grow without the water of life — love. You know this in your heart. To wait for this, rather than actively seek it in all ways is the greatest mistake. Don't succumb to this grand illusion.

Plants seek water. They develop roots and extend roots to where water is found. Do not wait for love to "happen." Start with finding it within your own heart, within your own being. Love is present at the very depths of the heart. The surface covers this love with concerns and hurts, resentments from the past.

As Evelyn Underhill says, "By the word *heart*, of course we here mean not merely 'the seat of the affections,' 'the organ of tender emotion,' and the like: but rather the inmost sanctuary of personal being, the deep root of its love and will, the very source of its energy and life."

Dear friend, we need but find a way to cultivate love. That is now available to you. Deep within. All that is necessary is a way into the True Heart, the innocent heart that radiates pure love.

The way in is easy. It comes with setting the mind aside. It comes with the music of life — a sound that carries one past the workings of the mind into that pure heart. This is meditation. This is Heart-based Meditation. Music takes you in the flow of life. It carries you out of the ego, if you allow this sound to go deep into your heart. It carries you to the source of love.

No one told you, dear friend, where the source of love is. Nor did they tell you how to contact it. It lies deep within your being. The entryway is through the heart, below the feelings. The method is very simple. Remember intuition, music and love are processed predominantly in the right brain. Sound and music can lead us into the silence to the source of love.

This is the foundation of growth. We must have a way to nourish love within ourselves. You have this within you. All it takes is a willingness to let yourself go and be nourished. It can be a simple turning within and letting go using a specific sound in a way that carries you into the depths. This is meditation. Meditation is the foundation for further growth. At each point in your story, as you came to see and know reality more, there was both input from the environment and growth of the nervous system.

To water and nourish the nervous system we need to do two things: Contact its source. Learn the skills that make up love, that create love. Integrating these two will be profound for you. Love is one of those abstract concepts. You can get into debating what love is and come to the conclusion that it can't be defined. But the skills that make up love can be. *And they can be taught.* What are those skills?

Acceptance, gratitude, forgiveness, compassion, appreciation, kindness, generosity, faith and caring, protecting and providing. These are the skills you will master as you grow. The intellectual understanding (left brain) works with the intuitive knowing (the right brain), and the integration of the two makes for rapid development. The two work in tandem. Just having intellectual understanding can lead nowhere. Understanding is half the equation. Doing is the other half, and integrating the experience is what is necessary for mastery.

I am asking you now to pause, to take a deep breath and to settle into the knowledge that your heart is being held and protected and that your life is being transformed to grace and ease. I write these words from my own heart, but with awareness of the lines of energy that stand behind me and ask that I reach out to you. You have been struggling with life far too much. You have been experiencing too much pain. You have taken your heart and have had to hide it, protect it, ignore its pains and walk through life longing for greater love. You have been afraid that you are not enough. You have been afraid that you are alone or will end up alone. You have been trying to juggle all the demands of life and it has been hard. You have not had the opportunity to develop mastery where love is concerned, because you did not know how to grow love.

My friend, know that it is not the strength of my desire for your ease, your joy, your total certainty that you are loved that inspires me to write. It is my great joy to tell you that if I can find this heaven on earth, so can you. I want you to be in love. In all ways... not just in romantic love with a partner. It is time for you to be awash in love. It is time for you to find such overwhelming heartfulness *for yourself* that your heart becomes brimming with joy and fullness.

❝

It is my great joy to tell you that if I can find this heaven on earth, so can you.

❞

I grew up hating myself. I felt dumber than my brothers, who were incredibly smart. I felt I was too skinny, my hair too curly and my face too boyish to be attractive to women. I felt I could not do enough to justify even my very existence. So, dear friend, if you have doubts about finding love, and if you have doubts about ease, let me tell you again: If I can do it, so can you.

I want you to experience what life is like when you feel love all around, you adore not just another, not just humanity, but when you adore yourself *and* your partner *and* humanity. I want you to find within yourself the keys to overcoming fear, grief, sadness, frustration and anger. I want you to find the keys to spiritual growth and development. And I want and long for your liberation from the cage we call the ego — from the programming and patterns that recur in life over and over again, and from the triggers and the reactions that keep you stressed and hungry for ease, peace and love.

You have the opportunity now to think outside the box and be outside the realm of the life you have known in the past. You must no longer wait for heaven. This is no longer a concept. When you exist in the field of love, in the fullness of love, in an ocean of love, you find a haven, you find healing, and you find heaven.

My friend, I am so sorry no one has taught you this. They did the best they could. They tried to talk about love and about its importance. They tried to tell you to love. They did the best they could. Yet, they did not teach you *how* to love.

They did not teach you how to live in love, and how to be in love. And so being in love became for you a special notion reserved for the special occasion — another heart resonating sufficiently with yours, so that your heart opened and found unity. So beautiful. But what they didn't tell you was that the beauty was not in the heart of the beloved, rather it was in *your* heart. And, very important, they did not tell you that the open-heartedness and the love and the unity you felt was not because of the person you were with.

You were in love because your heart opened to love and has found the infinite unity and bliss that is present in *itself* and in life — the infinite bliss and joy that is present in every moment in each part of the glorious universe, in each sunrise, in each sunset and in the eyes of every baby on the planet.

You were in love because you have let go of the mind and the longing to be somewhere else. You were in love, because you were in awe of creation — at that moment, the awe of another Divine being in creation — your beloved. But make no mistake: Being *in* love is not because of the beloved. It is your natural state. The fullness of love is the natural state of the human heart. And having your awareness in *that* fullness of love is also your natural state when you grow up and evolve. Then you are in the love of the heart. Then you live in love. Then you exist in love. Then you *are* love.

I want you to be in love in all ways. Romance is wonderful, but it is even more wonderful when your moment-to-moment experience is full of love, when you live full of love in your moment-to-moment awareness. Life becomes completely full and completely satisfying when you live in the experience of the heart's love with each moment. When you are in the love of the heart, then life is transformed — forever. This is what you grow up to. This is where you are headed. And restructuring the programming in both the conscious and subconscious mind is what brings an acceleration in your growth.

"

When you grow and evolve, then you live in love. And you know you are love.

"

So, be in love. Let me guide you to the wonderfulness of your tender heart. Let me show you the way to the awe that comes when life is lived in love. It is not a fantasy. You are enough. You deserve no less. We have several things to do before you can discover the truth of my words and live them in your experience. But we really have only one thing to do: Let go and discover who you really are.

Let us address love itself. Let us discover it and discover the depths of your heart. Let us address the fear that overwhelms the heart, the trauma, the pain, the grief, the sorrow, the anger that cloud and cover and make you feel that love is not real or just reserved for babies or cats and dogs. Let us be in the question of how love actually works — not what the religious texts or the spiritual teachers have taught but what *your* experience actually is. How does love work? How do you come to the core of the heart? How do you truly love?

First, start by honoring yourself. Honor the ways in which you have closed your heart. Nothing is a mistake in the true wisdom of creation — even mistakes! Honor how you have shut down and protected your heart and sworn you would never let yourself get hurt again. The heart is worth protecting. This protection serves you. It serves an important purpose. Thank it. You can have it and hold to it if you wish. But first, you must accept it. You must recognize and accept it, for it has served you well. If it hadn't you would not be here. It was only helping you to survive. Honor that wisdom that it has helped you to survive. Even if some other wisdom comes in, dear friend, and starts to count the ways in which closing your heart has limited you — honor the closing of your heart, for your heart is so precious, and love so important that you want to keep its tenderness sheltered. Whether hidden from others under an exterior of toughness or as a sophistication, too clever to be lulled into another relationship or another romance... Whether avoiding caring for a sibling who has hurt you or a friend who has betrayed you. Whatever it is, whatever the way you have kept a wall up — honor that first! It is there for your protection. Sit with it and talk to it and thank it for the way in which it has served you.

Acceptance is the starting point. If you are in resistance to what is, you cannot be in the love; you can't get back to it. So come to acceptance of what is. That which you resist, persists. That which you accept, you can choose to let go of. These are universal laws of the heart. The more you resist, the less energy you have. The more you accept, the greater the opening for new energy and new choices.

A story to clarify this: My youth was harsh because of my natural sensitivity and my having to learn to hide my heart. The coach on the swim team pushed us far past what our bodies could handle. Exhausted, I dragged my body out of the pool on the first day of swim practice. "Are you tired, Dugliss?" the coach asked. I felt like this was obvious, so I said, "Yeah, sure I am."

"WHAT??? Do two more laps." I had to swim more while the rest of the team sat in the bleachers watching and resting. The coach had made an example of me. A part of me was embarrassed. A part of me was angry. But overall there was just this sense of not belonging on this planet. What kind of a place is this where you pretend to be something you are not in order to prove something that is obvious — that you are a man. It was crazy.

So I learned to hide what was really going on inside. It was my only defense. I closed my heart, too, to men like my swim coach. Authoritarian, militaristic, conservative — I hid my anger from myself and made them different from me. Later in 10th grade when I was at a boarding school, I sat in a group with the football coach, who was one of the resident faculty advisors for the dorm next to mine.

The school was trying to find an answer to the rampant use of drugs by starting dialogues with the students about the issues and what drives kids to drugs. I was disrespectful to this man because of my past and my assumptions about coaches. When this was brought out, this football coach explained how he views his role as a coach and how he listens to his players and how he encourages them, rather than disciplining them. I realized I had judged him, and my prejudice blocked me from something very special. It was rare for me to find a man like this, who, with his warm, southern drawl and imposing physical stature, was truly kind and caring. I had closed my heart to something it had needed.

And then I did something that was even worse. I criticized and hated myself for being so prejudiced. I could not have tenderness towards myself for my mistake. I could not sit with the loss and come to a place of understanding and say to myself, "Paul, it is understandable after what you experienced that you would act this way. It is okay. Now you know. You did the best that you could do. The way these men acted was confusing to you. So, of course, you would close your heart. It is okay. I love you for wanting to protect your heart. I love you for enduring the discipline and the abuse. I love you for caring. And now you know you have survived, and you are here. You made it through, and now you are ready for something different. I love you for recognizing that and now opening to it."

No, instead I berated myself and made my encounter with Coach Walden a source of more pain. When I saw him after the discussion in the halls of the other dorm, his warm smile and caring hello was something I had a hard time taking in because it reminded me of the embarrassment from unveiling my prejudices. And so I missed a wonderful opportunity, not because I had closed my heart to all coaches, but because I did not honor the resistance that I had had. I did not recognize it and accept it and sit with it. I did not come to a different choice around it. I created even more resistance by resisting my resistance, and I turned that into self-hatred.

Today, I can laugh about this. In more recent years, I have joked that even my problems have problems. The unwinding of this comes rather easily though. Had only I understood or been taught the true nature of love, of the heart and of human growth and development, then perhaps I could have cherished my heart, its tenderness and my very pure innocence that had caused me to respond with honesty and integrity, "Tired? Yeah, sure I am."

For men, it perhaps does not seem like a very manly thing to accept our tenderness to such a deep level that we can acknowledge it and talk about it. This is because we do not understand that a real man has the strength to be completely vulnerable — to recognize the little boy inside and how resilient and enduring he is. Willing himself to greatness does not show the depth of a man's heart — finding the power of love and the strength that allows a heart to feel great tenderness and endure great pain and break through to real caring and mature love is what shows it. A man honors the courage to care.

For some women, it may seem too direct and confrontive to stare at the resistance and use the word honor — that may seem like a masculine, military concept to wear a badge of honor. Instead of the word "honor," perhaps the words "to hold space" work better.

Perhaps closing your heart has limited you. Perhaps it has kept the pain stagnant. Perhaps it has lowered the quality of your life and sucked the energy out of you. Don't judge it. First, feel the wall, feel the confinement, feel what is there. Bring your hand to it, and place your hand over your heart. Accept it. Observe it. Get curious about it. Become fascinated by it. And accept it. "Oh, this is what is there. This is what I am doing. Oh, wow, I can feel the wall! Amazing! I can feel the mind spinning around so that I don't have to feel what is there. Wow." Resistance is *natural*. Accept it. That is a major step to transforming it. That is a major step out of the suffering.

Gratitude

If the only prayer you ever say in your entire life is thank you, it will be enough.

— Meister Eckhart

Honor every aspect of life by giving thanks and gratitude. Giving thanks or thanksgiving is what moves acceptance to the next level where you find the goodness in what has been holding you back. Even honor the resistance. It *has* served a purpose. It *has* kept us safe. Thank goodness!

The unfolding of the heart and our full potential can be like peeling away the layers of onion. Or it can be like the unfolding and blossoming of a rose. One way on the journey to the depth of the heart is to be in constant gratitude. How amazing is it that you are here now after all that you have been through? How amazing is it that you still have a heart? How grateful can you be that your life is so graced that you can take the time to reflect on the status of your heart and come to acceptance? The path from acceptance to gratitude is a very short one. Thank goodness you are here. Thank goodness you have another opportunity to be in the love. Thank goodness you have survived. Thank goodness you have the wisdom to see and know yourself. Thank goodness you can see how amazing life is!

Dear friend, that takes quite a shift for you. Part of resistance is not wanting to shift. Just as I had resistance upon resistance, you will find yourself finding ways to *not* do this. It is okay. You will avoid it — until you don't. Seriously, you will avoid it until you don't. We all get to this point eventually. You can take as long as you want.

One of the things I have discovered is that growth is not about insight. It is not about thinking — it is about doing. Because this mind of yours and this ego of yours are so clever and so complicated and so entrenched, their mental and emotional habits are down pat. So any deviation from those feels inauthentic. "That's not me. That doesn't feel real. I can't do that. That doesn't work for me." Love that. Love the resistance by first recognizing it and accepting it. And do something different.

My craziness was that I expected that because of my insight, I could do the same thing, think the same way, and somehow magically things were supposed to change. That is the definition of insanity — doing the same thing and expecting a different outcome.

A wise man once said, we change not only by decisions, but by cultivating new habits routinely.

You are on a journey to the center of the heart, to the core of existence, to the discovery of true happiness and lasting peace, to the love that you have always wanted. These are some of the steps. You can take them when you are ready. Acceptance and gratitude...

I have been so impatient with myself and have been asking why I am not enlightened yet. How can it be? Now the answer is so clear. I am so grateful for my unenlightenment, for my resistance to change. I spend much of my days counseling people, advising students and encouraging them in their spiritual growth. My resistance and my emotional challenges, my sensitivities and my relationship challenges, my suffering and pain have led me here to this place of love and happiness. I could not be of service without all that I have experienced. I would not know about resistance and acceptance and the path to the core of the heart and to happiness without knowing this resistance. I would not come to gratitude without it. I would not come to love my tender heart, my sensitivity, my innocence and my integrity, if it were not for all that I have experienced.

You can't know what a diamond is and how it differs from glass without experience and knowledge. I overlooked the diamond and now can love my precious heart, my sensitivity and my innocence. It has been a long struggle. But I am so grateful for it has led to real happiness and to real love and to a fulfillment that spills over into all my relationships. Instead of being impatient, I now honor Grace's timing. And I recognize that I am increasingly more awake, more aware and more enlightened. I have had many experiences that people would call signs of enlightenment. Now I am content with the Universe's timing on all of that and on when the full enlightenment will dawn. This is contentment born of gratitude and wisdom.

The challenge of my sensitivity and my resistance to the way the world is brought me to meditation at the age of 18. If I did not fit in the culture, if I felt like I was from a different planet, this sealed the deal. I began to experience life very differently from others. It was the greatest gift in my life. Now I am grateful for the resistance and the challenges, for they led me to the heartfulness that I experience today on a daily basis.

I am so grateful to Grace for my dear heart. I am so grateful to each one who insulted me, the kids who mocked me, the ones who misunderstood me and thought that I was conceited, when I actually disliked myself and was constantly frustrated with myself. I am so grateful for the women who could not love me and forced me to find the real source of love. I am so grateful for being so weird and unconventional so that I was forced to go my own way. I am grateful for my shortcomings. I understand, dear friend, that this sounds strange. Never would I have you glorify your suffering. Never would I have you accept abuse. Never would I have you assume that life needs suffering. What I want is to show you the way out of suffering.

❝

Never would I have you assume that life needs suffering. What I want is to show you the way out of suffering.

❞

One of the jokes I love is about a man who falls into a huge pothole. It is twice as deep as he is tall. He can't get out. He sees a doctor walk by and yells, "Doc, can you help me out here?" The doctor pulls a pad out of his coat and writes a prescription and throws it down the hole.

Then a priest walks by. "Father, can you help me out here?" the man yells up.

"Yes, my son, I will pray for you." And the priest walks on by. Then a friend comes along.

"Friend, can you help me out here?"

The friend says, "Sure." And he jumps into the hole.

The guy yells, "What the hell are you doing? Now we're both stuck."

"Yeah," says the friend, "but I've been here before, and I know the way out."

Don't glorify suffering. Don't take a Pollyannaish view of it. Let me be your friend. You don't have to take as long as I did to come to this place of ease and love of life. There are shortcuts. One of those is to start to see how your challenges have shaped who you are. They helped you to develop character, to move forward and to come to this place where you are now ready to explore love more deeply than ever before.

You don't pretend. I understand. You aren't and really shouldn't be grateful for abuse and injustice, for ignorance and immorality. You can be grateful for the opportunity to learn from these, for the chance to take the high road, for the opportunity to strengthen your character and your resolve. You can be grateful for the blessing of knowing that you will never engage in these behaviors, for you have experienced the pain they bring. And you can be gracious and have gratitude for the challenge to the heart and how you have survived the challenge. The challenge has proved your strength. The challenge has made you know the incredible depth with which you can feel. It has helped you to know the incredible love you can embrace *because* you have been stretched… you are still here, and your heart can still feel. So, you can find gratitude in many ways without being insincere.

Take a moment, my friend, and reflect on the life of William Ernest Henley. With the stress and struggle of poverty in the late 1800s in England, he grew up with many challenges, and at the age of 26 developed tuberculosis that migrated to his legs. He had to have one of his legs amputated. While recovering he wrote this:

Out of the night that covers me,
Black as the pit from pole to pole,
I thank whatever gods may be
For my unconquerable soul.

In the fell clutch of circumstance
I have not winced nor cried aloud.
Under the bludgeonings of chance
My head is bloody, but unbowed.

Beyond this place of wrath and tears
Looms but the Horror of the shade,
And yet the menace of the years
Finds, and shall find me, unafraid.

It matters not how strait the gate,
How charged with punishments the scroll,
I am the master of my fate:
I am the captain of my soul.

This is the poem *Invictus* that inspired Nelson Mandela during his imprisonment in South Africa. "I thank whatever gods may be for my unconquerable soul." You have that. No matter how many times you have felt like giving up, your soul remains unconquered.

So take a moment, my friend, and just recite these words. There is no need to ponder any of this deeply. Remember change is in the doing, not just in the thinking. So do this, and see what your experience is. Just say these sentences out loud. Feel the charge behind them, and note the changes that arise.

Today I am here and present to my life.

I give thanks for my unconquerable soul.

I give thanks for all within me that has brought me to this moment.

I give thanks for life.

I give thanks for awareness.

I give thanks for strength.

I give thanks for my weaknesses and for those weaknesses I have had which are now strong.

I give thanks for those who have supported me along the way.

I give thanks for wisdom that leads me back to who I really am.

I give thanks for the wisdom and love that leads me back to my own true heart.

I give thanks for the beauty that is in the innocent smile of a child, the face of a baby, the affection of a dog and the sight of my friend's eyes.

I give thanks for being able to be aware of feelings and for being aware of when the feelings are blocked.

I give thanks for the enduring strength that has brought me to this moment and for the feelings of weakness and overwhelment, which I now know were only part of the story.

I give thanks for all that I am.

I give thanks for all that I will become.

I give thanks for every perfection and every imperfection.

And I give thanks for the one who has been able to know and do all that I have done.

And I give thanks to my dear, innocent heart.

I give thanks to my dear, tender heart.

I thank the one who has experienced all of this.

In the name of all that is, I give thanks.

And so it is.

Gratitude is a powerful portal into love and higher consciousness. It is the key to abundant living, and it is a powerful component of happiness. But it is not the only way to journey to the core of the heart.

"

Gratitude is a powerful portal into love and higher consciousness.

"

Forgiveness — Making it Sacred

For the person who has learned to let go and let be, nothing can ever get in the way again.

— *Meister Eckhart*

Honoring and accepting what is opens the heart. Giving gratitude for what is warms the heart. Making what is sacred connects the heart back to its divine source. You make it sacred by giving it over to the Divine. When you make things sacred, you sanctify them, you sacrifice them. Sacrifice is not a slaughtering. It is a "making sacred." You do this through a process called "giving over" or what some call "forgiveness." Forgiveness is an emotionally charged word and perhaps not the best, for it is associated with this egoic self-righteousness that says, "I will come down from my throne and grant you pardon even though you were wrong." This is the common association with the word. Instead, real forgiveness is letting go and giving over to the Divine. It is not mine to judge.

When I hold on to my judgment, I fix the thing to me. When I give it over, I say, "This is yours to handle, not mine." There is no longer any judgment or any righteousness. It is given over to the Divine. It is a complete letting go.

You accept. You give thanks. You let go and turn it over to the Divine. You forgive. Then you celebrate. You celebrate the glory of grace, the beauty of freedom, the joy of life. In the process of grace you find the joy in it, and then you come to love. All of these are facets of love — all are doors to the core of the heart. Be blessed with that.

A human being has so many skins inside, covering the depths of the heart. We know so many things, but we don't know ourselves! Why, thirty or forty skins or hides, as thick and hard as an ox's or bear's, cover the soul. Go into your own ground and learn to know yourself there.

— Meister Eckhart

You can practice many things. But there is an important piece — to come straight to the core. To come straight to love, you let go. You let go of the mind and go directly past the finest feeling level of the personal heart straight into its core — straight into the divine heart. You do this with true meditation, as well as letting go in daily life.

Forgiveness is paramount in the journey to the core of the heart. It is a letting go. You practice the habit of letting go with meditation. With conscious practice of forgiveness and giving things over, you become free. The path to the core of the heart becomes easy and open. Forgive and let go. Then all freedom dawns, and you come to know pure love.

"

Forgive and let go. Then all freedom dawns and you come to know pure love.

"

Faith and Fear

Faith is taking the first step even when you don't see the whole staircase.
- Martin Luther King, Jr.

Faith is the strength by which a shattered world shall emerge into the light.
- Helen Keller

The answer to fear is certainty. Certainty that you are safe. Certainty that you are loved. Certainty that your lover will be there. Certainty that you are worthy. Certainty that you are connected to a higher order. Certainty that things happen for a reason. When that certainty is not apparent — when the money, the job, the lover, the connection has not yet manifested — being certain that it will manifest is what is known as faith. You don't know how, you don't know when, but you know that it will. Faith is the aspect of love that is the antidote to fear.

When I was working with Aureya, she mentioned that there was still fear left in my energy body. The events of the last few years prior to our meeting had left me with all kinds of uncertainty. Job, career, spouse, friendships — all had shifted dramatically. At the time I was single, and the fear that I would end up alone in life was present and easily recognized by her acute intuitive abilities. "What you radiate is what attracts the partner to you. Not any attempt for you to control things by acting a certain way," she said. "Radiate your essence — the intelligent, spiritual man that you are — and the partner will come."

Like so many surface fears, the deeper fear lay underneath. The fear that I was not enough or that my actions had accumulated such karma that it was not in the cards for me to have a partner in this lifetime. I still held the fears from childhood that I would not be known or accepted for who I was. Each of the many fears that remained lodged in my energy system needed to be brought to awareness and healed.

I found healing these fears was a process that resulted in the certainty born of faith in what was yet to unfold. I had had enough experience to feel confident that if I were sued for malpractice that I would always be able to find another career outside of medicine. I had changed careers enough times and had no one depending on me, so I was bold enough to go without malpractice insurance when the rates skyrocketed in the early 2000s. The fears that lurked deep within the subconscious mind seemed most related to love.

As I worked with Aureya, she would look into the programming that seemed to be lodged in my energy centers or chakras, and often the origins would go back into past lives. We focused on a event in a past life — the loss of my beloved and children due to an army of bandits while I was far out in the fields, able only to look back at the house burning in flames. My wife was my match, my ideal love, and our blissful years together were all gone in an instant. I would seek her and fear losing her in several subsequent lifetimes.

To heal this meant first becoming aware of it and then pulling it into a space of honoring my former self and what I had endured. It required coming to a space of love in my own heart for that former self, and bringing an awareness that the trauma does not need to continue on. It is done. My task was to bring the situation to awareness, bring love to the former self, bring wisdom of what was learned, and then completing the lesson and letting go of the old energies and finally allowing a new pattern to be established. Time and time again Aureya took me through the release of the old patterns through the healing power of awareness, wisdom and love. Love heals and paves the way to wholeness. Out this wholeness comes the strength and the certainty that leads to an unshakeable faith.

"

Love heals and paves the way to wholeness.

"

I am focusing on the emotional body because the feeling level of life is so intimately tied to the heart and to love. And love is the fastest path to enlightenment.

Each emotion arises out of love and leads us to greater love, if we *learn* how to relate to the experience of it — how to digest and metabolize emotional experience.

Love is a path in itself. Fostered by the Divine and the angels' love, it can lead one to the highest development, the greatest joy, and the pure, true, and real happiness. It requires mastering emotion. It requires a shift in mental perspective and outlook. And it requires knowing the source of love, knowing the silent field of bliss at the deepest point in the heart. This can only come through meditation, a meditation that allows you to experience the subtlest, finest feeling level and go beyond it into the ocean of silent bliss and love deep inside the heart. The task is really threefold:

1) Cultivate your connection and experience of the source of love, the silent center of the heart through a Heart-based Meditation practice.

2) Heal your emotional body so that the programming and patterns around emotional pain can be released and returned to love.

3) Learn love. Learn to think with your heart and love with your mind.

Heal the emotional body, dear friend. Fear, sadness, grief, frustration, anger are all manifestations of the pain that comes when we are wounded and have not found a way to heal. Heal yourself. Love yourself. Love the world. And reside in love.

You have done so well to get to this point. Yes, there has been pain. Yes, you may feel damaged at times. Yes, you may have developed self-destructive patterns and behaviors and done things you regret. But you are here, in this moment, and, if you let yourself, you can feel my love for you. Here, in this moment, you can choose to heal and for your life to transform. Here, in this moment, take the next step in your growth. So much has not been what you expected. So many times you were challenged. But here, in this moment, you need only come to be present with what is present in your emotional body.

I know you have experienced great fear. We all have the fear that we are not truly loved. We all have the fear that we are not enough. We all fear that life will be over too fast. And in our weaker moments, when the pain is great, we all fear that life will never get any better.

Let me comfort your fears now. Give them over. We all have them. Acknowledge these fears as real. Don't use the mind to deny your experience. In your experience it is very real. I want you to know and accept what is real *for you*. The greatest confusion and problem we have is when spiritual teachers and leaders speak from their level of reality. "Oh, your fears are just assumptions that your mind is making. They aren't real."

No, my friend, your fears are very real until you heal them and outgrow them. When the spiritual teacher tells you that fear is not real, it is like a professional basketball player saying that to dunk the ball, you just run up to the basket and jump. That is what *they* do. To say that to a child is to mislead them. A child hasn't grown tall enough to just run and jump and dunk the basketball. Your fears, my friend, are very real. Spiritual progress has been slowed too much by making it something to bypass reality. "I am universal energy, and I am everything, so I have nothing to fear." That is only true when you have developed yourself to be free of all the old programming and patterns and have integrated love and awareness.

You don't grow by escaping. You don't resolve karma by escaping. You don't attain higher consciousness by escaping. When you run to the ashram, your ego gets there first. It has already planned out how it is going to be so wonderful in this spiritual environment and how fast it is going to evolve and how blissful it will be. Anyone who has spent time around the great gurus knows that the ego gets there first. All of the egoic conflicts and problems are intensely heightened in the ashram. Everywhere you go, there you are — until you aren't. That is, until the "you" that you think you are is transformed, and the soul runs the show.

                ❝

When you run to the ashram, your ego gets there first.

                ❞

God didn't create the universe so that she/he could hurry up and escape it. It is there for us to enjoy. We have forgotten how to do that because we have forgotten how we grow. We have forgotten how we resolve karma. We have forgotten how we grow joy and happiness.

Dear friend, you grow through love, through experiencing repeatedly the *source* of love deep within yourself. You grow through love by learning how to cultivate it, expand it, live it and be in it. Be in love — this is the way you grow.

Know that the body has a structure that holds it together and keeps it going. Similarly, the emotional body has a structure. Without getting technical, the energy of emotion comes from the physical body. If we give you a shot of adrenalin, you will have an emotional experience. You actually have an energetic body that is the interface between the physical and the emotional body. The point is that emotions are not just in the mind. They are anchored in the body. So you must locate and become aware of their seat in the body if you want to heal, digest and metabolize these into their pure essence — love. Locate the fear and where it resides in the body.

This concept of energy and digestion may seem foreign. Emotions represent energy that can be stagnant or flowing, unchanging or transformed. When emotions are held in the body, they get stuck, and transformation is difficult. Holding the emotion in place also takes energy. Yoga is designed to move or digest these and further your growth and enlightenment. For now just come into awareness of the body and where the emotion resides, where the fear lives. Feel into it.

Remember this, dear friend, everything has a purpose. Every experience, every feeling has a purpose, even your fear. And the fear's purpose always begins with trying to help you to do something. Maybe your fear was something you learned in childhood when it was *not* safe. Maybe your fear is protecting you from trauma or humiliation or loss of love. Maybe your fear is distracting you from your pain. Maybe your fear is distracting you from anger that would destroy your success or your relationships. There are so many possibilities.

Fear serves us. It protects us. It distracts us. It motivates us. Here is the key: *Love the fear.* It is serving a good purpose. It has been invited by your soul for your learning. Come to the love in your heart. From the standpoint of great love, love the fear. Give gratitude to it. Once you understand its purpose, let go into gratitude and thank it.

For years, I tried to overcome my fears, feeling they were a problem. This style of repression forced me to have to process the fears in meditation, and while it did create a greater will and strength, it did not serve. It slowed my growth, rather than accelerating it, and made my meditations very busy. Avoid the mistake I made and let yourself give gratitude to the fear and discover its purpose and give thanks to it.

Recognize as you do this, two important things happen. First, you come into an awareness that you are not your fear. You are able to identify with the love that you are and less with the fear that consumes you. You come to know yourself as separate from the emotion, instead of experiencing yourself awash in the emotion, as if you were the emotion. Instead, there is the emotion, and there is you.

Second, you now have the chance to choose. How do I want this fear to operate in my life? Do I still need it to be running the show? Can I assure it that I have learned my lesson and that I don't need it to hang on so desperately? Talk with the fear that you have. Love it and praise it for what it has done for you in the past, even if it is outmoded in the present. And then ask it to work with you in a different manner.

This is coming into love. This is loving what arises. This is being in love. This is the way to relate differently to any fear that pulls us out of love. This is the way to relate to any fear that consumes our experience and turns heaven into hell. This is easy when it is practiced and when it is combined with deep meditation to remove the stresses held in the subconscious mind. But this is very hard when you first start. Why? Because the tendency is to skip two important steps. The anchoring in the body and identifying where it is located is key to releasing the energy that holds the emotion in place — that holds it in the subconscious mind. You need to be sending energy and awareness to it — sending love to melt it and release it from its moorings.

Next, you need to be solid in identifying with love as you approach the fear and talk to it. Growth and enlightenment are a process of shifting experience out of identification — shifting out of being consumed — whether it is emotions you identify with or thoughts or physical sensations. Here is where freedom lies. If you don't anchor into the feeling of love and identify with who you *actually* are, then you identify and are consumed by and are lost in the feeling. Then you get lost in your judgments about the feelings. "Oh, if I only weren't so emotional…" "If I only could beat this depression…" "If I could only stop being so angry all the time…" "If I could only grow up and stop being such a baby and being afraid of everything…" Then you judge your judgments and identify with *that*.

Dear friend, let it all go. Come into love. Let fear be your ally. Love your fears. Love your experience and how intensely you can feel them at times. Meditate and practice loving your fears, so that they no longer consume your existence, and so that you can identify with what the mystics call "reality." You are the love. Be in yourself. Reside in love.

Love is more than a bunch of words. It comes out of the silence. Words express its movement. Love is more than a feeling. Love evokes a feeling of warmth and comfort and draws you to it. But it is not feeling. It is more than that. It is more than energy. It arises out of the silence and is at the core of the heart. Meditation is a journey to that core. Reside in love. Meditate. Strengthen the core of love in your heart. Dip into the Source of Love deep within — carry this out into life, and be in the love. With that, watch everything in your life transform. Watch all fears lose their grip on you, and watch every moment become a glorious play of love and light. From this vantage point you will develop an unshakeable faith.

Dear friend, it takes tremendous courage to be human. It takes tremendous courage to acknowledge and be aware of the fears we hold. What it takes is worthy of recognition, of praise, of acknowledgment and honoring. Each human being has endured and survived so much, so very much, just by the nature of our existence. We have an exquisitely sensitive nervous system that can hold great pleasure and that can signal great pain. Somehow, in spite of all of this, we come back to the truth: Through all the trials, the fears, the trauma, you are still alive. You have made it through. And you have the ability to come back to love, time and time again.

I love every hesitation, anxiety and fear that I have ever had.

I love the way these have given me the experience of life and have guided me to this moment, where I can take fear and discover wisdom, and I can face fear with a loving heart.

I love this life, as difficult as it may have been, for it has guided me to Grace — it has motivated me to find a way that is easier and more fulfilling.

I love each fear and each anxiety.

They show I am precious enough to worry about.

They show I am important enough to care about.

I love each moment and how the fear comes and then intensifies and then lessens as I listen to it and talk to it.

I love this life.

I love these fears.

I love this heartfulness.

I love myself.

And I now reside in love.

Sadness and Grief

Dear friend, sadness, grief, loss are so difficult. Fear gives you a visceral shock to wake you up to danger. When you digest that, it wakes you up to a greater feeling of aliveness and a greater love of life. Sadness and loss are very different. They stand in the way of us enjoying life. They create such deep emotional pain and can stand in the way of love. Sadness reverses life; it undermines the life force, and it can lead you into the darkness of depression. It comes from you having invested so much of yourself into something only to lose it. Don't judge it. Don't be afraid of it. Love that you care so deeply. Love that you are having this experience of the depth of your caring and the depth of your heart. Love the one who grieves.

Understand that all that is so deep in the heart and the pain that you feel are letting your heart deepen. And as Meister Eckhart says, "Truly, it is in darkness that one finds the light, so when we are in sorrow, then this light is nearest of all to us." The light is there. Just one minor shift: Come into the love for the one who is sad, who has lost, who is unable to feel the energy or liveliness for life. What your sweet heart needs in these moments is your deepest love. Be in that love.

Dear friend, sadness is part of the grieving that comes when you let go of something dear to you. All too often what you are letting go of is the mind's illusion about the world and the future:

"I thought I would have an easy relationship once I was on the spiritual path."

"I thought I would have great abundance once I started to visualize my perfect job."

"I thought I would be without emotional pain, once I began to love myself more. Instead, now I am sad."

As you let go and stop projecting onto the future, you create the opposite illusion:

"I will never have an easy relationship."

"I will never have great abundance."

"I will always be with emotional pain."

While our tendency to use a crystal ball and predict the future is inherent in the mind's thinking, the situation is not just mental. You are releasing the emotions and the beliefs that no longer serve you.

This is the direction: You let go and you allow life to present itself to you. You let go and allow. You don't know what will happen. You can be grateful for this "not knowing." Life can be a wonderful surprise when we allow it to flow. Sadness will only stick to you if you get wrapped up in the illusion that you can know the future, and you are certain that it is *bad*. No one knows the future. And you don't need to know the future — if you can let go of the fear that it will be bad. Come back to loving yourself. In that moment you let go of expectation and let go of the future and come to right now, and you find your heart is always available to you. You always have that available to you. Your heart and your heartfulness are always available to you.

Grieving is the process of letting go. You usually don't want to let go. You care, and that is a good thing. The judgment placed on "attachment" as something nonspiritual is misleading. That is for the monk who is away from society and who is trying to detach from everything. When you care about something wholeheartedly, this can be just as spiritual, if it is done from a place of pure love.

The transformation comes in raising love to its highest expression. If you are hoarding old newspapers because you are attached, and that attachment represents your security, then little room exists to let love flow. You are not loving and caring of newspapers. You are hoarding out of fear and disconnection with the flow of the Divine and the order that appears in all of life.

Raising this up means letting go of the illusion that these newspapers will make you secure. You love the one who is afraid and feeling insecure. You love the fear and the need for certainty. You let go of the notion that collecting things will make you secure. You let go and allow yourself to love being human and to find security in higher things. You can love newspapers for their content and well-written articles and thus feel the draw to something higher. But you let go and grieve and understand that caring and attachment are part of being human. You don't want to be uncaring. But you *do* want to let go of illusions that bind you.

Sadness shows you care, which is a good thing. Persistent sadness shows you are caught in a mental framework that is not consistent with reality. You must come to restructure your thinking and beliefs. It is important that you care. It is important that you have things, concepts, values, people and pets that are dear to you. And it is important that you be able to let yourself love yourself for your caring.

From there, you can come to loving whatever unfolds. Yes, the world may disappoint you. But recognize that your happiness is not in what you are letting go of. Happiness is in *you*. You can let go of something or someone, because you always have the kindness and tenderness of your own heart and of the Divine's heartfulness for you. You always have that. That can fill the gap. Reclaim hope. Reclaim caring. Let your life force flow again. But this time flow it back toward the one who cares as well.

❝

Happiness is not in what you are letting go of.
Happiness is in you.

❞

Dear friend, understand that sadness is a natural process. It is a natural way to release and let go. The tears that follow the release are the hardest part of the letting go process. You need to divert the energy that you placed into the hope, into the attachment to the idea or the person that you now must let go. Mostly you are letting go of your emotional and energetic investment, which is the most difficult. You can get so stuck in the process and the competition between hope and acceptance. You can go back and forth.

Come into the space of loving the one who hopes. Fill your heart with love for the tenderness of your own heart. Fill yourself with love for the one who cares. As you fill yourself full, then you begin to identify with that fullness. In fullness, the loss does not hurt so much. In the supporting environment of your own heart, the sadness does not need to be so deep. It becomes a cloud that passes over the sun — but only for a few minutes. Dear friend, love the one who is watching the clouds come and go. See the beauty of the sky, clouds and all. And be blessed with the awe of life.

I am grateful for this moment.

I am grateful for this moment where I can stand back and observe my sadness.

I am grateful that I can feel it.

I am grateful for my pure heart.

I am grateful for the tenderness that I can feel for this.

I am grateful for the love and compassion that I can feel for myself.

I hold onto the love.

I give my tenderness to myself.

I give all graciousness to myself.

I reside in love and let this flow to the sad and painful parts of myself.

I reside in love.

I reside in knowing that my love is always there.

I reside in knowing that love is always there in spite of my sadness, my loss, my grief.

And I love myself.

And I love myself.

And I love myself.

Dear friend, in all that is experienced as a human being there is a blessing. It is not a simple strengthening and tolerance of pain that is being cultivated. Pain is your signal that something is out of tune — that it is time to let go into greater love.

The angel walking next to you says, I am witnessing a loss of love and a loss of wholeness that throws you into greater pain and greater suffering. The karma is not knowing how to negotiate life and find that inner peace and that inner calling. In all that is to unfold for you, stay with us, and stay in that inner peace, and relate to that inner peacefulness. In all that is to unfold, your angels and guides will be right with you, and they will bring all that there is to be in the fullness of all that can be.

Let go of pain. Let go of sadness. Find glory in the life that is present. Move into action, and make each person's life better by radiating love and by doing something special for them.

It is in letting go that all comes to being and all comes to good. This is not the ego getting good at controlling things by letting go. This is practicing letting go and going out of the mind. Normally the mind is so absorbed in the thoughts and perceptions and experience of the ego that it is even hard to recognize the Being that is experiencing it. When you step out of the mind into the awareness of the body, into the awareness of the feel of the body, into the energetic body, then suddenly your consciousness is not absorbed and identified with thought and with the mind. This is one way of letting go. This is energy work that aids evolution.

There is another way. It is to let the mind become absorbed in a sound that trails off until the sound disappears. This is meditation that hastens evolution. These practices separate out the identification and take us to the state of Being — to pure consciousness. These practices enable you to let go. The more we practice them, the easier it is to come to Being.

There is yet another way to practice letting go, and this way has side benefits. It is to come into the pure, innocent heart — into the spiritual or universal heart. Taking our attention to the center of the heart and feeling the pure love that is there fills us with love, bliss and awe and cultivates not only the letting go, but also the bliss value that is present in our existence and often hidden from view.

So, step out of your mind and enjoy the greater fullness of life. Live the love, and keep your light shining brightly.

Part 3

Intuition - Thinking with the Heart

Jan & Aureya - Intuition

The second thing Jan taught me was intuition. What a gift! I had never felt myself to be intuitive or psychic or clairvoyant in any way. I had a lot of doubts when we started. She gave us a quick task to demonstrate that we had more intuition than we realized. This opened the door to two days of instruction that allowed me to begin a daily practice of tuning in to the Higher Self — a practice that became part of my daily routine, which I continue to this day. Jan taught that the aspect of us that is the Higher Self is a part of the Divine — is an aspect or part of God. "We don't test God," is what she emphasized.

The small self or ego wants to doubt and challenge, to claim responsibility for how great it is that it can intuit. It wants to feel like it won't be duped if all this intuition stuff is an unreliable hoax. All of this stands in the way of Pure Intuition. All of this creates a testing of God. God does not need to prove anything. God already knows. God has nothing to prove and will wait patiently until you are willing to approach with respect. It was a key element to overcoming my over-intellectual, over-analytical and often doubting mind. "You don't test God."

It did take practice, as Jan said it would. But it opened up a whole field of possibilities and connectedness that I never would have otherwise experienced. Unbeknownst to me, I was cultivating the integration of one of the important functions of the right brain. It is also the third key of self-development — developing an internal guidance system.

Integration of greater awareness requires reprogramming mental-emotional patterns. It requires a way of moving subtle energies and integrating higher-frequency energies into your subtle body. And it requires an internal guidance system. Why the later? Because the age of gurus is passing. The age when the full development of the human nervous and human potential was reserved for an elite few who could find their way to an enlightened guru — that age is over.

It is the time when full development is to be widely known. Guidance is needed along the way — and not just general advice. Specific guidance for the individual is needed for the current step that you are on. That being said, we have entered an age where placing all trust in an authority and following by blind faith no longer works. It is a time when this guidance is to be found inside of yourself. It is a time to develop the inner guidance system. For some, this is connecting to their intuition. For some, it is connecting to their Higher Self. For many, though, it will be connecting with their guides and angels — something I was to learn much later.

It was actually a couple of decades later that I learned to use my intuition for something more than guidance from my Higher Self.

I never thought that I was particularly intuitive or that I would be able to develop my psychic abilities to any extent. This was a curiosity to some, as they could see my third eye was open, and they did not understand my lack of experience. Much later I came to understand that it was important that I not use these abilities extensively. I made certain agreements to safeguard their proper use. Now that I understand the setup, I can understand how the abilities "show up" when they are needed.

Again, I get a bit ahead of myself. What I want you to know is this: You have within the guidance you need. Intuition will take you where you need to go. But you need to cultivate it. My friend, you have it within you. You have more wisdom, more knowledge, more guidance, more sage advice *than you ever imagined.* Have confidence in the knowing that your soul and your Higher Self are guiding you.

Aureya spoke of the transition in life, as you shift from the ego running the show to the soul being in charge. The transition can be sharp and disruptive — the whole life can be turned around. When it is time to wake up and become enlightened, then the ego is often shaken out of its role of control through all sorts of betrayals and reversals and a ripping away from attachments. It is not a requirement, but it is a common experience. Some call this the dark night of the soul. It is really the dark night of the ego. It is the soul's daybreak.

The dark night is not necessary. You can come to the soul gradually and easily and with grace. It is through fulfillment that the heart becomes so full that the ego can let go with grace. It is through the power of peace and the power of love that the chains that bind the ego to its ways and its control can be released. A new way of life and a new freedom dawns.

❝

Some call this the dark night of the soul. It is really the dark night of the ego. It is the soul's daybreak.

❞

In this process, the guides and angels around us can serve a valuable function. They can lead us to ease and grace and the way forward. It was through Aureya that I learned to see and sense and connect with my guides, which opened the path to the angels.

The key with intuition is to recognize that it comes from a different plane of life. It is right brain, not left brain. It comes from a region *outside* of the mind. What does the ego do? The ego uses the mind to doubt and test and try to verify the intuition. "Not 'til you become like unto children can you enter the kingdom." Intuition requires the mind to quiet, and the innocent, pure awareness to be present to *whatever* appears. This process is greatly enhanced with meditation.

You are to let go of the mind. Doubt undermines the process. What is presented, just is. That is all. No evaluation, no testing, no doubting, no wondering. These are all coming from your mind. Love with your mind. Don't test and doubt with it. Your heart knows, my friend. It *knows*. You may call it a "gut-feeling," but ultimately it is the heart that knows, that decides and that guides.

You have such treasures within you. Each day of life is a miracle. Unfold that miracle through letting go of the mind and coming to the pure heart. You have great knowing available, if you will listen to it. You have within you a wonderful energy and a propensity for grace, ease, fun and happiness. Just listen. Listen to the heart, and make it your guidance system. Intuition is available to you. It is present within you. Set the mind aside, come into silence, and allow impressions to come to you. At first these may seem chaotic and strange. But, as you listen more, you will come to know what the messages mean. You will know what is your intuition speaking and what are just random thoughts in the mind. Silence is the key. Pure consciousness is the key. Innocence is the key.

I learned quickly to sense when it was intuition talking. The mind has for me an airiness. Intuition has a warmth and a groundedness. It has a solid sense of knowing. It is like knowing your name. You just *know*. I remember walking into a drugstore. I was late for a class, so I was in a rush. I had just had a great meditation, and everything was so very clear. As I entered the store, I was amazed at the light and the glistening of the reflections of light off of the rows of products. There were so many rows. I never realized the store was so huge before. It was more like a grocery store than what I had associated with drugstores. I needed two items: dental floss and scotch tape. No clerk was to be seen. How was I going to not waste time finding these?

"Oh," I thought, "I will just use my intuition." Dental floss. Out of the silence: "Four aisles over, midsection." I went there and bingo, dental floss! Now, tape. Out of the silence: "Two aisles over, front section." Bingo! I did not will it to be so. This is so very important — "I" did not do it. It came to me. "I" was not involved. All "I" did was get out of the way and go into the silence. I created the space for the knowing to come through.

When you give over to grace, then you come to understand, my friend — you don't *own* gifts — they come through you. Because it is the nature of the world to be manifesting gifts. The greatest of these gifts is love. Love comes through you. You don't *own* it. The same is true with intuition.

You have greatness within. You need only make the switch from thinking with the mind to thinking with the heart. It takes practice. It is part of the integration of awareness. It comes in its own time. But it does come with practice.

The mind is a great calculator and evaluator. It is a horrible guidance system. Your mind can go from pro to con to pro to con and back and forth until it is totally confused. Your heart knows. Reserve your mind for loving. Use your mind for gratitude, for forgiveness, for kindness, for caring, for accepting, for loving and expressing that love. Use the heart to guide you, to decide, to know.

Think with the heart, and love with the mind.

You Are God

How would your life change if you knew this for certain? How would you treat others differently if you knew with absolute certainty that they were God? I know with all certainty that you are God, having the exact perfect experience that your soul came here to have. To know that you are God with full certainty and to perceive the depth and profundity of this knowing — the implications are unfathomable. If only everyone knew this. I have always had a deep respect for others, but now I understand why.

But there is more. Many spiritual seekers have this knowledge, but they couch it in terms:

"There is a part of me that is divine."

"Outside the ego lies the spirit."

"Everyone is God playing a role, but I haven't awakened to that yet."

And so forth. I realize now that even the ego is God, a creation of God for the experience of being human. It is not that a part of us is Divine and the rest is a mess. Come into the realization that God wants to have exactly the experiences that are being had, ego and all. Like some of us who like to see adventure movies or horror movies, it is all God wanting to experience everything and discover God. The more lost God gets, the greater the joy at being found.

I am God. You are God. Everything about us is God, which is why the angels honor and serve us so willingly. It is hard to express the shift that comes when you know that deeply, as opposed to intellectually. It is hard to express the shift when you embrace that ALL of it is Divine. In coming into that knowing, there is a presence and a love that is supporting each moment.

What To Do

Dear friend, I hope I have inspired you. I have presented some very abstract concepts. Ultimately, my words are meant to uplift you and to let you know that so much more is possible. You don't get there overnight. Growth does require some attention and focus. But it does come. Life is transformed. It does not transform by thinking about it. It does not transform by flitting from one spiritual interest to the next. It comes by and through love practiced and applied.

Learn to contact the source of love deep within your own heart through a self-transcending meditation practice like Heart-based Meditation. (See the resource section for more information.) Make this practice a part of your day like brushing your teeth. My dear friend David had a rule for himself that he would not eat until he meditated that day. Use this powerful tool with that kind of commitment, and it will amaze you.

Learn to remove the blocks to success, power, connection and love through working with the body's subtle energies and clearing the blocks to energy and the flow of Source love. This is done with energy work or by learning a type of yoga designed exactly for this purpose: Healing Light Yoga. (Again, see the resource section for more information.)

Understand that in every moment love is available. The word love may seem too tender for some. Love is power. Love is energy. Love is joy. Love is abundance. In every moment you can find your way to the power and presence and joy of being alive. It rests deep within you. Whenever you have the opportunity during the day, come to the true depth of your heart. Ask, "How can I bring more positivity, more light, more love to the thoughts I am thinking?" In each situation and in every dilemma, ask, "What would love do?" This is a powerful habit to develop that will never misguide you.

Powerful questions take us deep into wisdom and provide the platform for the next stage of growth. "What would love do?" is one of these most powerful questions. If you make this your habit in each and every situation, your life will transform.

An ancient Buddhist text says:

> The thought manifests as the word,
> The word manifests as the deed,
> The deed develops into habit,
> And the habit hardens into character.
> So watch the thought and its way with care,
> And let it spring from love
> Born out of concern for all beings.

Turn your thoughts to greater positivity, to greater love. Make this your habit, and create a new destiny.

Learn how to develop your intuition. Develop your inner guidance system. The Divine has given you it for a reason. Everything in society favors the mind and takes you away from your inner knowing. Let all outside of you go. Turn inward. Just like meditation, make tuning in your daily practice. Take steps each day to further develop your intuitive abilities. Take courses in intuition, such as the Energetic Mastery courses I teach. The more in tune you are with your Higher Self the more life flows effortlessly, and the more you feel supported by the Universe.

What else can you do? Begin each day with gratitude. This pulls energy and blessings and good luck your way. It sets you into a space of love and loving life. It cultivates and reprograms the mind. It serves your higher good in all ways. And it feels good.

Finally, each day set the intention to learn something else about love. No one gave you an owner's manual for your heart. At least not yet... that may be my next book — a workbook to accompany this book. Until then, explore love, and learn all you can about it. It is the most important thing in your life. It is better to not assume it "just happens." Open to the concept of learning the qualities and skills and the methods into love, into a bigger heart and into the greatest joy. Learning love will bring you benefits over the rest of your life. It is so important. You cannot find a way out of suffering until you find a pathway to the true heart. When you have learned to think with the heart and love with the mind, you have found that path.

Know this: Love heals. Love enlightens. Love works. Live love, and keep your light shining brightly. And may you be so blessed.

❝

Live love, and keep your light shining brightly. And may you be so blessed.

❞

Resources

Meditation:
www.heartbasedmeditation.com

Healing Light Yoga:
www.healinglightyoga.com

Energetic Mastery / Intuition:
www.energeticmasterynow.com

Dr. Paul Dugliss:
www.drdugliss.com
www.pauldugliss.com
www.newworldayurveda.com

Aureya Magdalen
www.aureyamagdalen.life

Jan Kinney
giwspiritjan@icloud.com